••• ISSUE 007 •••

Buckman Journal

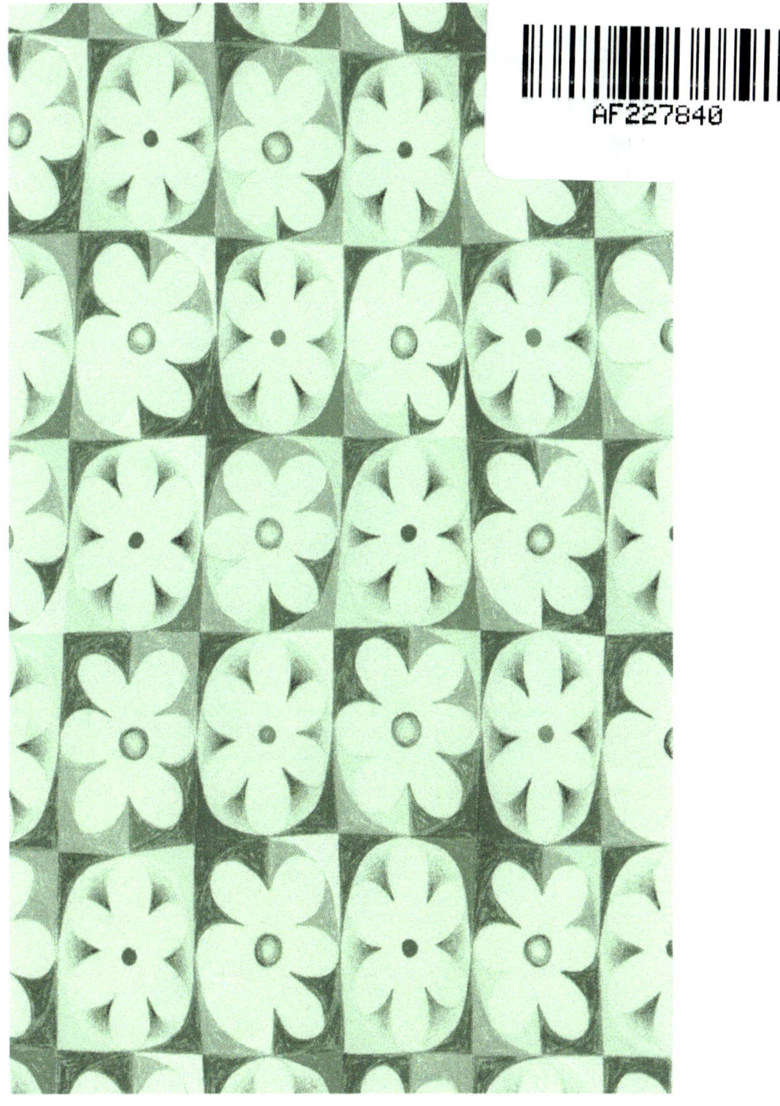

Portland, OR
buckmanjournal.com | Buckman Publishing, LLC

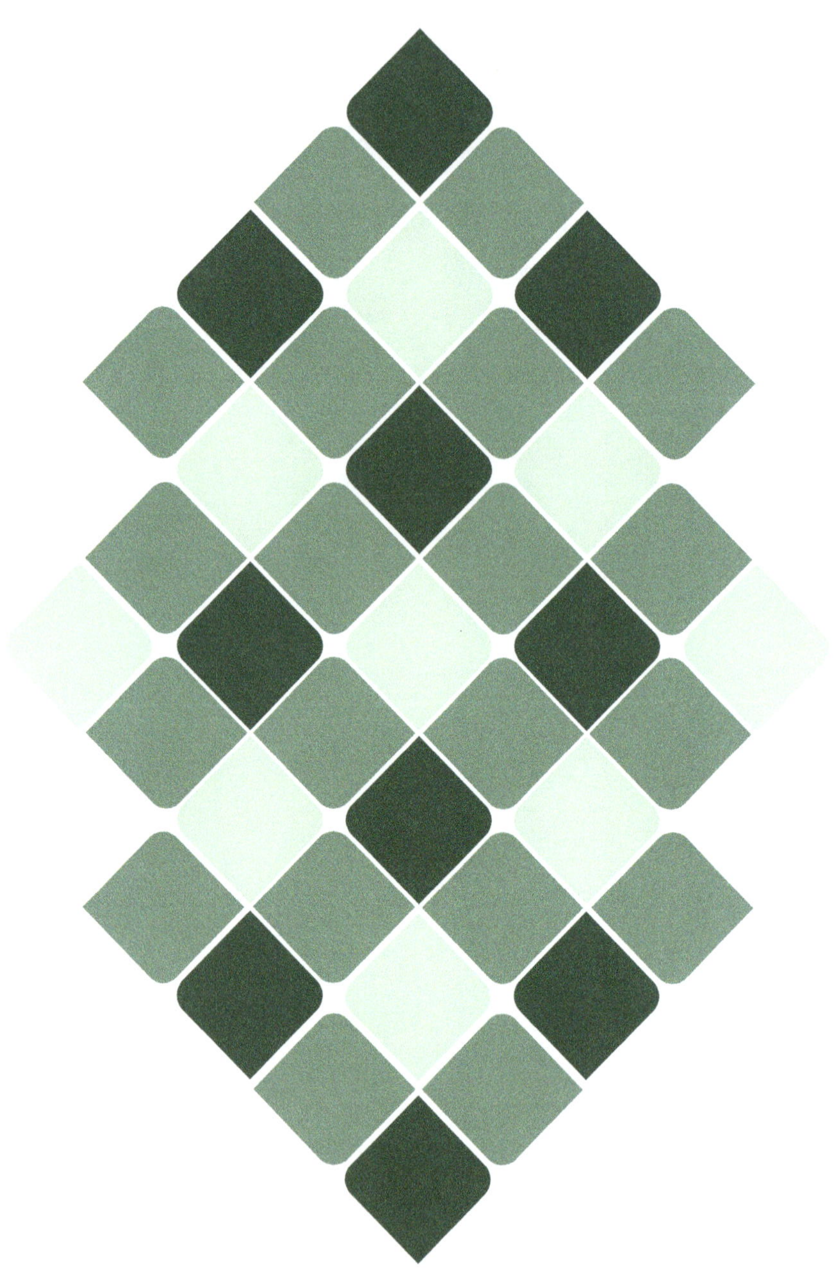

Cover art by: Tomás Oliveras.

The Buckmxn Team

Buckmxn Associate Rich Perin is mostly invisible.

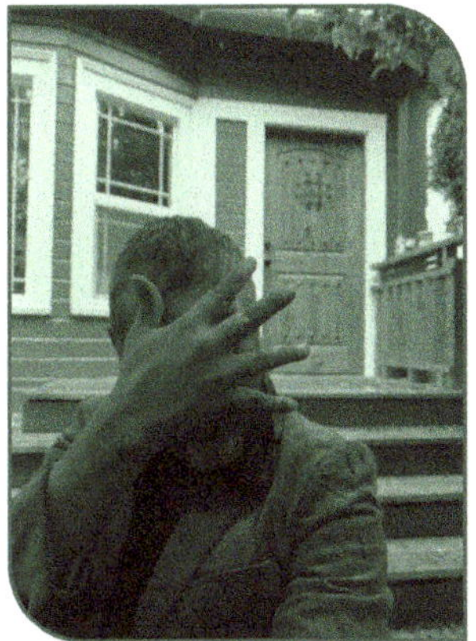

Editor Jerry Sampson (she/her) is a screenwriter, freelance writer, horror writer, film analyst, screenwriter, and Editor of Buckman Journal. She writes for *Ghouls Magazine*, *Rue Morgue*, *Moving Pictures Film Club*, *Vague Visages*, *Horror Obsessive*, and other horror sites. She has released a book of short horror stories entitled *The Scream & Other Dark Stories* through Buckman Publishing. Her love for film and the horror genre leads her to explore and question the darkness that lies in the shadows of human existence.

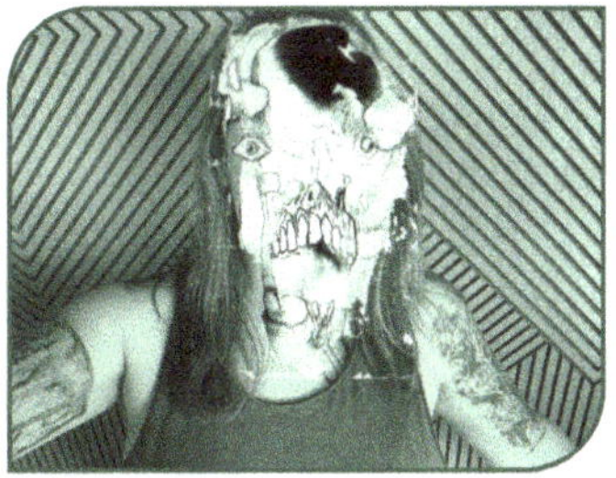

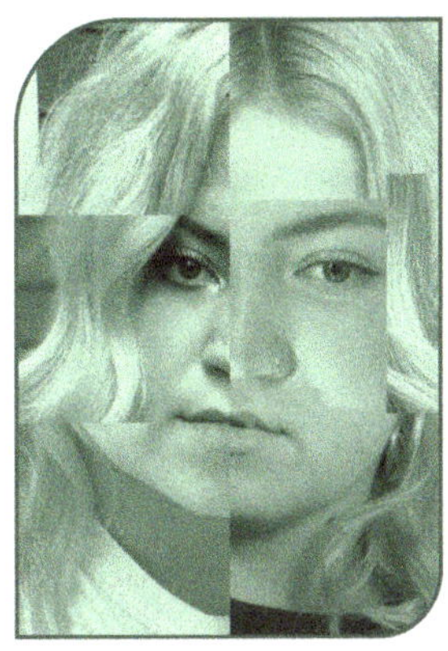

Designer Hannah Johnson (she/her) balks at every opportunity to talk about herself, but reluctantly will share that she's a designer and illustrator hailing from the Pacific Northwest and, in spite of her rainy upbringing, embraces heavy-handed use of color in any application. She will also embrace any dog, any time. You've been warned.

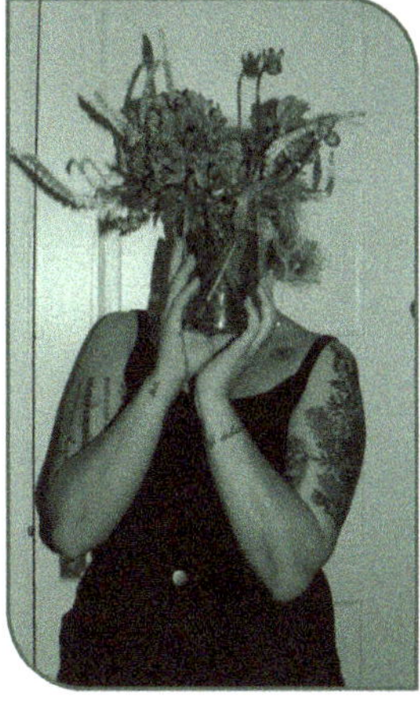

Operations Manager Emmi Greer (she/they) is a poet, educator, and hybrid-genre artist. she is forever obsessed with the polyamorous relationships between language, art, and consciousness.

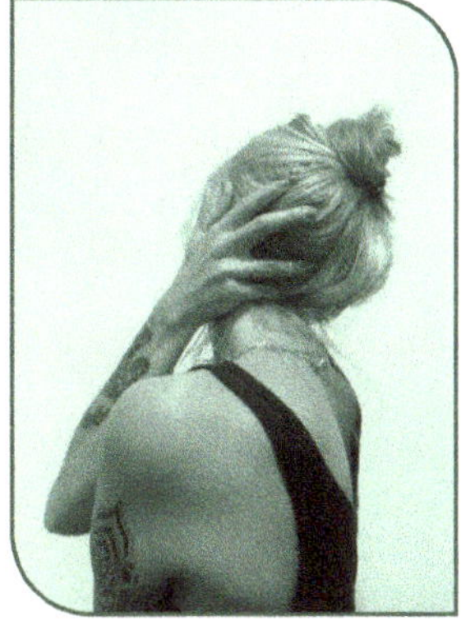

Art Director Ellen Robinette (she/her) finds it equal parts vexing, funny, and challenging to write about herself as someone who expresses with visual language. She occupies the space between artist & designer, with an overarching interest in material qualities. She frequently enjoys eating in bed.

In This

RUNAWAY CHAIN

Words: Jerry Sampson

Art: Kyle Wallace

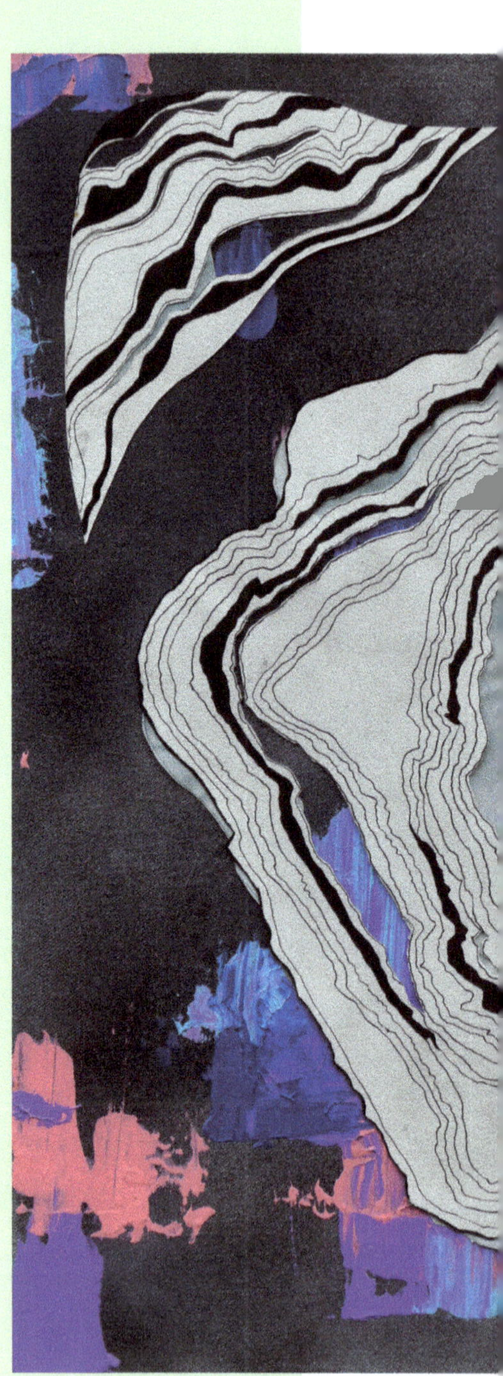

Kyle Wallace
(he/him) likes to make things— better and worse with his hands rather than a computer. Kyle hopes his work elicits mood more than anything: elevator paintings with an idea that's neither demanding of attention or muzak.
Instagram:
@cale4niapizakyle

01

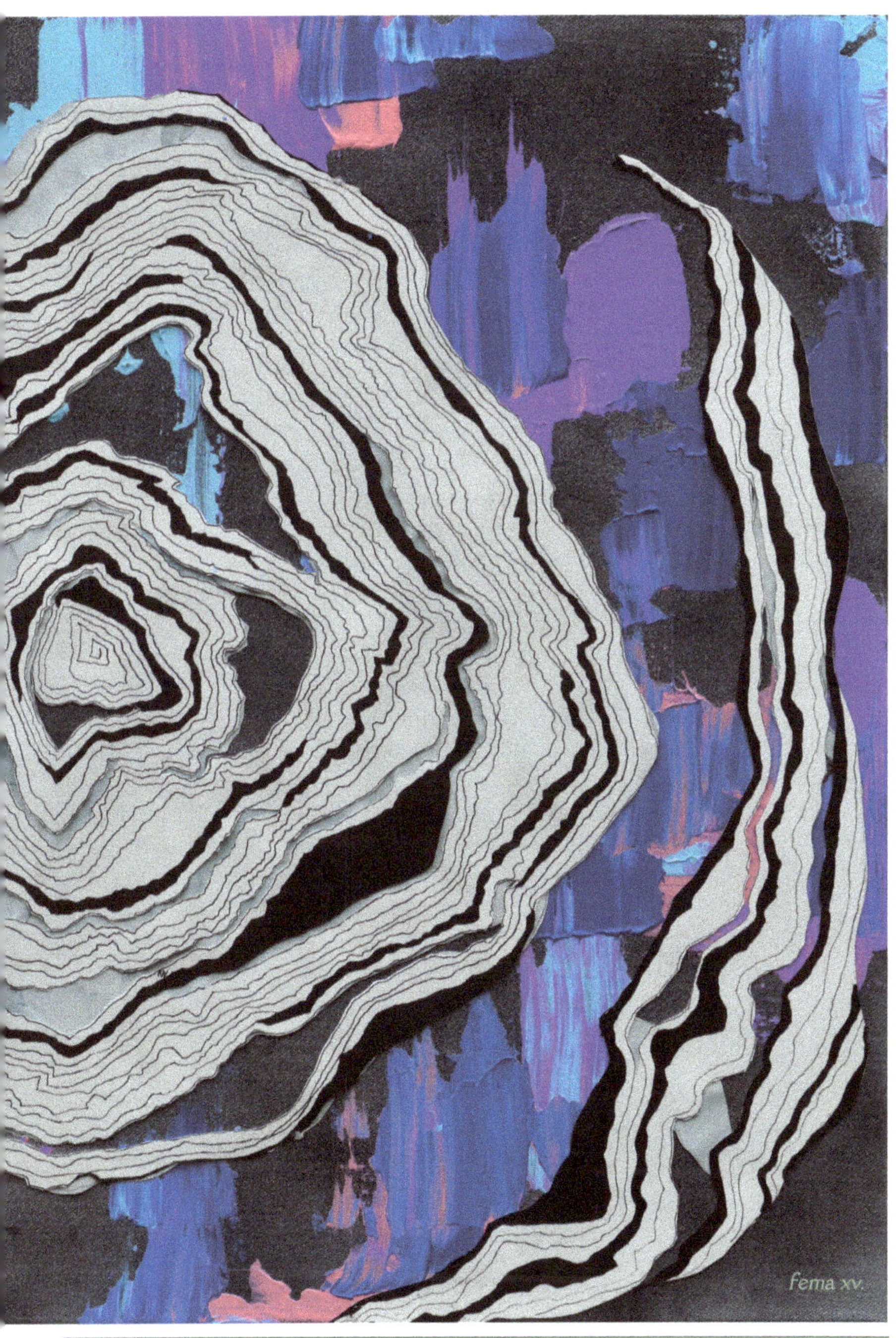

DAY 001
AWAKEN

I can't open my eyes.

White-hot light surrounds me, lining four walls that I can't see, but can feel. Murmurs from a crowd fill the space; a buzzing that quickly turns deafening. I try to remember where I am, who I am, who *am* I?

My mind is blank. An empty screen showing static.

Bringing my hands to my face, I force my eyes open with fingers that feel completely disconnected from my body. Through a murky blur, I begin to adjust my mind to what I see. I try to stand, but quickly realize that I am being weighed down by a thick, silver chain.

Silver? Metal? Is it cold on my ankle?

Awash in terror, I release the breath I have been holding with a long, shuddering sigh. A claw-like hand wraps itself around my mouth, cutting off the sound that I am beginning to emit.

I close my eyes again. *Please wake up.*

DAY 002
UMBILICAL

I feel a tugging on the chain and then a warm hand covers mine. The hand is attached to an arm, a shoulder, a neck, *my face.*

Impossible. Not my face, but a face that looks like mine, but its eyes are a deep purple. Are my eyes purple? No, my eyes are blue.

Without moving its lips, It speaks to me.

Time to wake up.

The tugging at my ankle returns and I see that my chain is attached to Its chain, and Its chain is attached to another's. This one also has my face, but with an alien quality. Not alien to It, but alien to me. Small nodules that look tiny mouths open and close on Its face as It stares at me with scared eyes. And the one past It, a neck so long it stops and bends at the ceiling.

We stand up, attached to one another, the line goes on and on. So many Me's, all so terrified and, with a strange sensation, I can feel the fear that runs through the chain. I understand that I am connected by more than these shackles.

A Shadow steps under a bright light and slashes through the air in silent proclamation. Our heads snap up in unison, not wanting to miss a thing.

The instructions are: When we walk, we walk together. If we fall, we fall together.

I lean towards the warm one with purple eyes to ask It what is happening, but all I get is a finger on the lips – *quiet.* I rub my eyes with the heels of my hand. I want my family; I miss things making sense. At one point we are told to wait, to sleep and prepare for the show. We have to sleep standing up, because it takes so much to move.

One of us at the front of the line asks for food. The Shadow immediately passes over It and the chain clatters, empty, to the ground. A murmur erupts from the belly of the group, but the hungry one is gone, swept away by an invisible hand.

I cannot stop my tears. I can only keep them quiet.

DAY 003
BACKSTAGE

The ones that call themselves Auntie pick us all up after snapping us awake. I slept but am not rested. I am set on a seat in front of three blinding lights as Auntie rubs lotion on my naked scalp. I wince at the burning that comes from the cream.

In my mind, a screaming takes over as one of the other Me's is taken by another Shadow. It happens more regularly, and each one of us that is taken leaves an inky blackness in Its wake. I feel that a part of me has been snatched away.

Auntie seems fearful of the Shadow too. And each time It passes, she draws her lips up over her teeth, shiny and white and impossibly cruel.

She leans forward and whispers in my ear. "What a beauty. There are so many here for *your* show. What great potential."

Her breath is a sour stench that crawls down my spine. We all rustle in our seats, together but so alone. It's a fear that is tangible, and settles in my empty stomach, along with the realization of what my future holds.

Auntie stands me up and presents me to the Shadow. It nods, and with a jagged nail, hits a hidden button on my chain. It hangs, weightless in the air, and at once the connection with my others is gone.

Before I can adjust my emotions to the newly gained freedom and loss, a door opens.

DAY 003
THE RUNWAY

Bulbs flash and burst, blinding me in an instant. I can't open my eyes, and I feel blood rushing down my face. I don't cry or wipe away the red tears. I step forward, one foot in front of the other, onto the runway – or whatever in this place it's called – and put my fate into the hands of the highest bidders.

I was told to smile but can't feel my lips, so I approximate what a smile would look like and trust that I will appease the Shadow enough to remain in the light. I am still more terrified of disappearing into nothingness than whatever waits for me with the unseen Lords that are bidding on my newborn soul.

My intuition tells me to stop and I do. Right at the edge. Excitement fills the room. Cameras and voices continue to blaze around me until a single Voice rises above the rest.

I have been claimed, and identity rushes through me. Individual, unique. My fear dissipates and a gust of wind blows through me. I open my eyes.

STAGES OF A FIRE

Words: Jason Arias

Art: Arthur Hitchcock

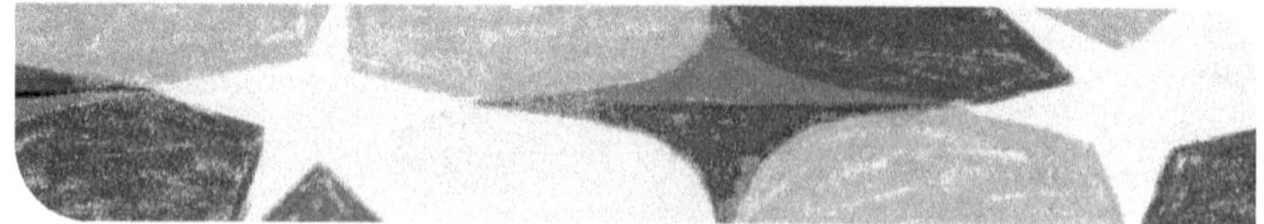

02

Jason Arias (he/him) lives on the Oregon coast. His debut short story collection, *Momentary Illumination of Objects In Motion*, was published in 2018 by Black Bomb Books. Jason's stories and essays have appeared in *The Nashville Review, Oregon Humanities Magazine, Harpur Palate*, Lidia Yuknavitch's TED Book: *The Misfit's Manifesto*, and multiple literary magazines and anthologies. For links to more of his work please visit **JasonAriasAuthor.com**.

Arthur Hitchcock (he/him) is a multidisciplinary artist and producer. He was born in the Midwest, grew up in Long Beach, CA, and is now living and working from home base in Portland, OR.

Incipient

(The initial stage in which a spark is ignited. The fire is easiest to put out at this stage and may even self-extinguish. Fuel, heat, oxygen, chemical reaction, structure size and flow paths are all critical variables for continued growth.)

Alyssa did not expect to be up at 3:30 a.m., at the Plaid Pantry on 162nd and Division Street, in the passenger seat of her brother Chino's twenty-year-old 1999 Ford Escort. But here she sits, shotgun, waiting for Chino to figure out how he is going to *quench his grand munchies thirst.*

She's tired. Exhausted really. So tired that once home she hopes to sleep the rest of the day, hopes not to awaken cotton-mouthed and feeling guilty about napping and biding time and everything else. Guilty about going to another escalating party that she's beginning to understand may never really end, until the day it finally does, grinding to a halt. Or worse: a fading, aging, dullness. Guilty about returning Dion's flirtations, even though she knew he had a girlfriend, even knew his girlfriend—but Trina wasn't right for Dion anyway, he was too sensitive for her, yet still. Guilty about *not having any inkling to initiate her higher education* like her school counselor had rightfully accused her of that last year of high school. Guilty about her dreams and the absence of them.

Alyssa can see Chino's head appear and disappear as he stalks the aisles inside the convenience store. Behind the floor-to-ceiling glass her brother's white wifebeater and black windbreaker bounce with his stilted gait. Alyssa knows that *wifebeater* isn't a term she is supposed to use, and because she isn't supposed to use it, she finds herself always plugging it in to conversations. Especially since Sheila had instructed her not to, back in junior year. And Alyssa had informed her that some wives did get beat, and that the acknowledgement of that fact was not an endorsement of it. And not all people that beat women (wives or otherwise) wear those shitty little shirts; her mother's boyfriends hadn't, for example, and yet... But Alyssa hadn't gone as far to say that last part.

If Alyssa could go back in time to her junior year, at Centennial, she would further correct Sheila Saltzman and her coven of uppity ups with the insight that their language (or disapproval of hers) didn't matter. That it never would. She would have broken it down into ghetto proverbs to make it crystal clear that shying away from vernacular didn't change the reality of anyone's situation. She would have...

Jesus, what is taking Chino so long?

Her tiredness is turning sour.

All the good vibes from the conversation with Dion are dissipating. If she doesn't see her bed soon her mounting irritability will keep sleep at bay for hours (the sunrise being an insurmountable obstacle to conking out behind thin curtains) and Alyssa can't handle insomnia right now. There are things to do. There is always something she should be doing. But what?

She'd already made enough mistakes for one twenty-four-hour period. They were small enough. Silly really. Forgettable. She was old enough to understand that mistakes would be made. That was essential. But it was the snowballing of mistakes (one, following another, conjuring a third, incanting a fourth) that

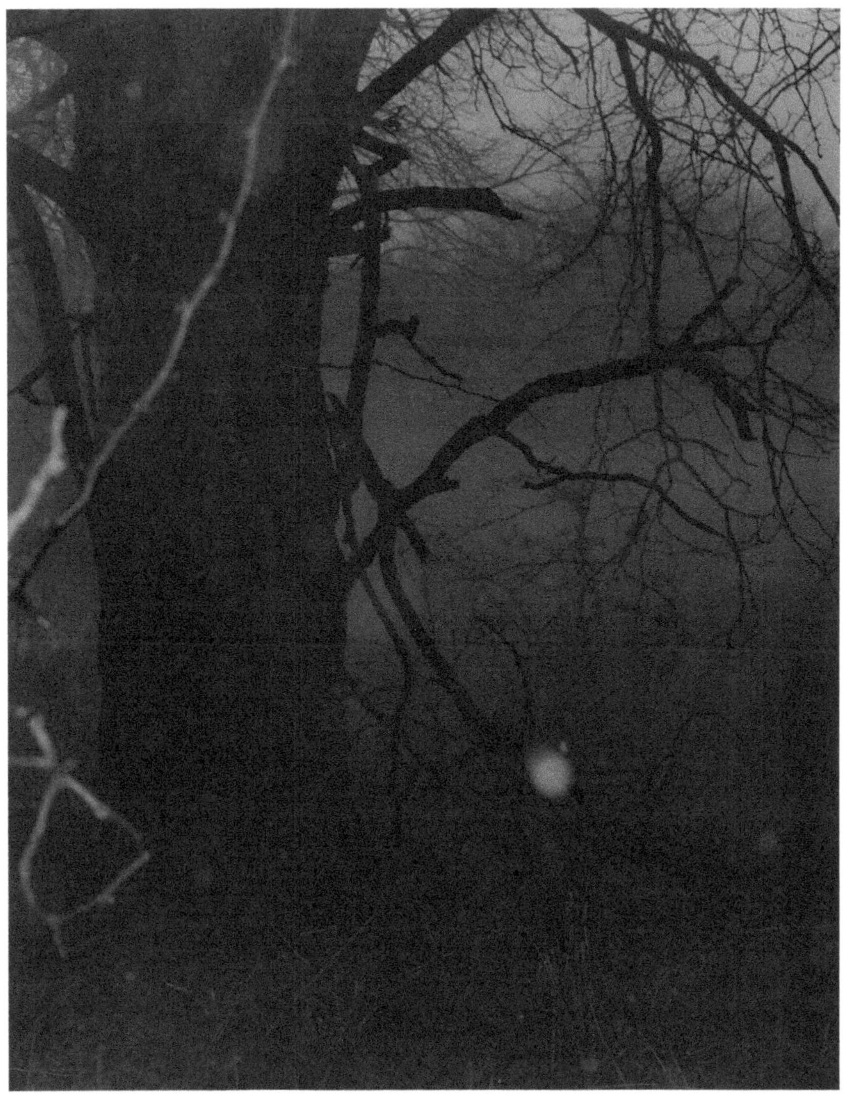

Recollect #1.

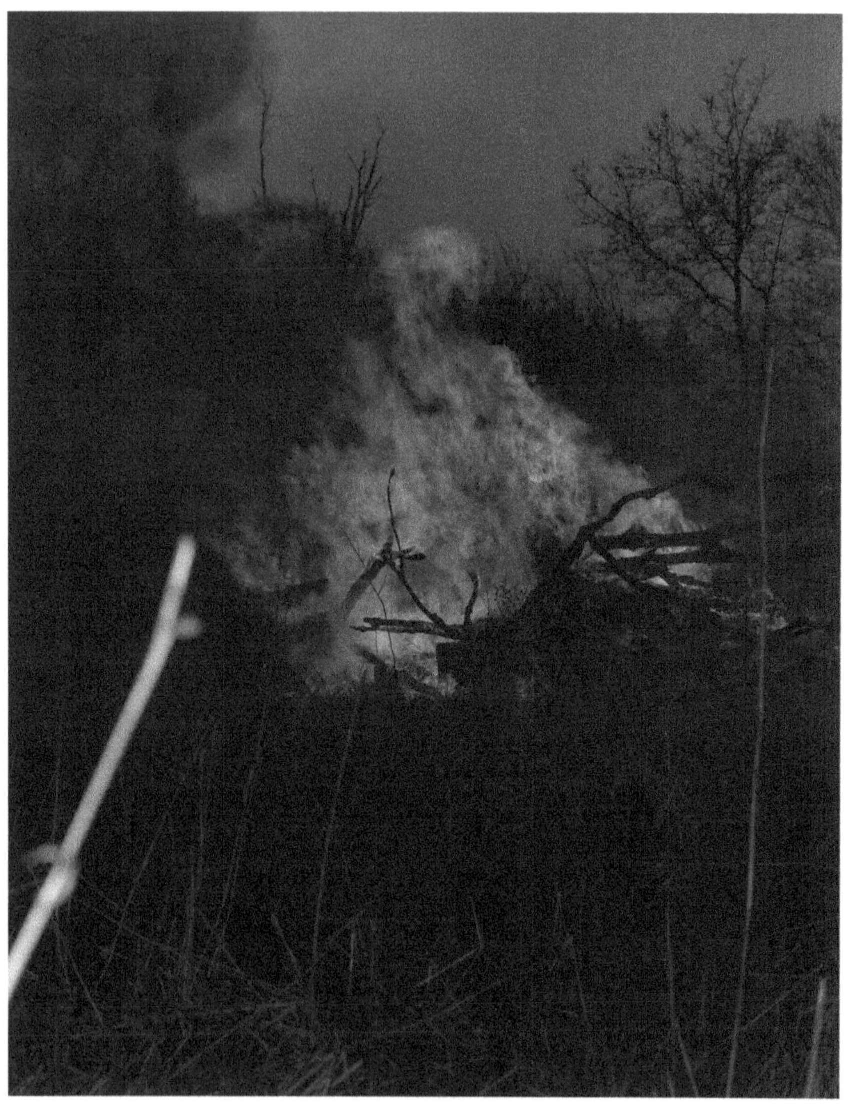

Recollect #2.

created irreversible futures.

Remain calm. Stay positive. Words only uttered in last ditch efforts.

Alyssa runs the palms of her hands down the thighs of her jeans with an even pressure, like trying to wipe away an invisible film. She stares at a stale fry on the Ford Escort's floorboard between her shoes. She rolls her head from side to side before opening the passenger side door and swinging her newly scuffed pink Converse into the parking lot. Her Converse had been spotless at the beginning of the night, but she kept stubbing her toe on thresholds while traversing from the yard to the innards of the party, kept spilling drops of drinks. Plip, plip.

Inside the Plaid Pantry, Alyssa finds Chino gesturing back and forth to himself in the candy aisle. His lips are moving, but only whispers come from them. Self-mutterings really.

Alyssa knows this is only an exaggeration of the way her older brother has made pressing decisions all his life. Though most of his soliloquies are much less obvious. Normally, candy isn't a pressing issue for Chino but, being coupled with exhaustion and intoxication, it is clearly becoming a distracting factor.

The cashier behind the counter (who looks like he could be anywhere from 29 to 45 years-old; just one of those white guys) has a newspaper opened in front of him but he isn't reading it, his eyes are trained on Chino's every move.

Normally Chino wouldn't let the cashier watch him. He'd be staring right back. *Never allow yourself to be watched,* his motto since copping it years ago from one of the older true gangsters in the neighborhood. It's a motto maybe even more helpful for young women than old gangsters and their young proteges. Eye contact was important. Most people are voyeurs: they just want to watch; they don't want to be watched.

"Good evening," Alyssa says to the clerk while nodding in his direction, trying to gain his attention, trying to pry his eye. If Chino saw the way he was being watched...

"Yeah, evening," the cashier says, looking at Alyssa for a second with his eyes, not his head, then pulling his eyes back to her brother.

"Or is it morning?" She ventures.

"What?" the clerk says, still assessing each of Chino's movements.

"It's just... is it actually evening or morning?" Alyssa says.

"Both," the cashier says. There is nothing she can say to lighten the air.

Alyssa walks past the cashier to the candy aisle where Chino is standing. She uses her body as a barrier between Chino and the front counter as best she can. She stands so close to Chino that she can smell the smoke and the drink from the night clinging to his clothing, overpowering the Tres Flores in his hair. She bats the side of Chino's Dickies with the back of her hand. "Chino, get the fucking Snickers already."

Chino pauses in his self-reflection at the half-wall of candy, turns to face her. His eyes are red-red. She hadn't realized how wasted Chino was until now.

"Oh, sure," Chino says gesturing to the shelving in front of them, "Snickers simply satisfies. But..." bringing his finger to pontificate at the side of his mouth. "The Butterfinger's textured crunch is on a whole 'nother level of deliciousness shit." He pauses with his finger on his chin. "And that's the dichotomy we have here, dear sister: if simply being satisfied is enough." Chino smirks. Maybe he isn't as far gone as she'd first assumed. Who knows? He spoke the same either way. Chino: the Latin American version of a neo-Shakespearean caricature clad in bandana. The strangely elegant coupled with the elegantly strange.

"Hey, man!" Chino yells towards the cashier, over Alyssa's shoulder. "Is there a reason you're looking at my sister's ass?" And this was also Chino: not so elegant, prone to aggression and mood swings, frustrated with eking out an existence in a world he found continual irony in.

"Oh, please, *Homeboy*," says the cashier, "don't make this into something it's not." He closes the newspaper he wasn't even pretending to read. "Look, do you plan on *buying* something?"

"What makes you so sure I'm *your* homeboy? Do you even know the etymology of that word?"

"What?"

"Well, let me elucidate. There are two roads we can go down because, like most of history, the origins are still being debated. One reference point for *Homeboy* is: *a term of endearment from one African or Latino American to another male from their homeland*. The other origin points to *an antebellum houseslave*." He finger-quotes his definitions. Chino snuffs his nose with one hand, grabs the waistband of his pants with the other. "Now, *cashier-boy*, in which way are you addressing me with this term? With appropriation? Or condemnation."

"I'm using it in whatever way that allows you to buy your candy and move the fuck on," he says, pressing down on the counter with both hands. "What? You think I need this shit from you? How old are you anyway? You think I'm scared of *you*, Homeboy?"

That's how fast some fires are lit.

That's how quick the right environment can combust.

Looking back Alyssa would swear the next sixty seconds happened in slow motion. But that's just the way memory is, it turns everything into a movie.

Dim the lights.

Skip the previews.

Run the reel.

Chino: Grabs a candy bar (not a Snickers) and throws it at the head of the cashier.

Cashier: Ducks below the counter.

[The candy bar bounces off the window behind the cashier.]

Alyssa: Pulls on Chino's left elbow towards the door. "Come on, let's go. Now!"

Cashier: Rises from behind the counter with a cordless phone in his hand. His head is cocked in a silent warning. Fear eyes. Fire eyes. Something else eyes.

Chino: Pulls a handgun from his rear waistband with his right hand. The gun is gunmetal grey, it is the most solid thing in the store. Chino aims the barrel level with the cashier's head. Shakes his own head from side to side slowly. "Does a man have the right to take his time when deciding what snack food to put in his mouth."

Cashier: Stares at Chino, open-mouthed.

Alyssa: Still pulling on the arm that Chino isn't holding the gunmetal grey gun in. "What the hell? Don't do this, Chi. Don't you dare!"

Chino: "Hey, *Cashier-boy*," snuffs his nose again, "does a man have the right?"

Cashier: "I don't know, *Homeboy*." Dead stare. Deadman's stare. "Does he?"

Growth

(The shortest stage, in which the fire load and oxygen fuels the flames. Factors include where the fire originated, nearby combustibles, ceiling height, etc. It's in this stage that victims can become initially injured or trapped due to flashover.)

Alyssa: Behind the wheel of the 1999 Ford Escort, quickly backing out of the parking space in front of Plaid Pantry. [The windshield wipers are accidentally knocked on. Fast wipers. Slow wipers. No wipers.] She turns the Escort onto 162nd street northbound. "What the hell? What the hell? What the fuck, Chi?" Swiveling head from side to side. "Idiot!"

Chino: Holding his gun in one hand and wringing the heated barrel with the other hand. "Could have shot that motherfucker. Why didn't I shoot that motherfucker? Where have my words gone? Why am I talking like this?"

Alyssa: Guns the Escort through the red stoplight on Division.

[Two cars on the street: one east of 162nd, one north of Division.]

Alyssa: "You mean you weren't trying to shoot the window behind him?"

[Blue lights illuminate businesses in the shopping center on 162nd and Division. The storefront of Subway bathed in blue. Rite Aid bathed in red. Cricket store, Liquor Store, Ace Hardware, and Ross all bathed in blue and red. The colors never blend. Never make purple. The progression of a cop car speeding through the shopping center parking lot.]

Chino: "I don't know what I meant to happen." Looks in the sideview. "But I'm afraid it's time to reach deep inside and pull out all those GTA evasion skills you've built on over the years, Lis."

Alyssa: Looks in rearview. Hands at ten and two. "Have you ever seen me play that shit, Chi? Jesus! Jesus."

[The Escort hooks a hard right on Lincoln Street. Hits the chicane. A quick left, a quick right. Hard left at the tee into 160th. Right at the ell onto Harrison.]

Chino: "No GTA, huh?" Body leaning hard left. All teeth grin. Big eyes energized. Head on a swivel behind and to the sides. Momentary hand out the passenger side Escort window.

[Flash of gun metal in the streetlight. Bushes rustling.]

Alyssa: Full brakes. Full stop. "Go get the gun."

Chino: "Lis, what the fuck?"

Alyssa: "Some kid's going to find that. Go get it."

Chino: Smiles big while revealing the disengaged clip. "No bullets in it. I can't have kids on my conscious, Lis."

[Blue lights illuminating the corner.] Escort makes a left on Mills. All the way across 148th. Blue lights are coming from north and south on 148th. Half a clip of loosed bullets thrown into blurs of bushes. Left on 143rd. Second half of bullets thrown at twenty-foot-tall arbor vitae. Left on Division. Blue lights are coming

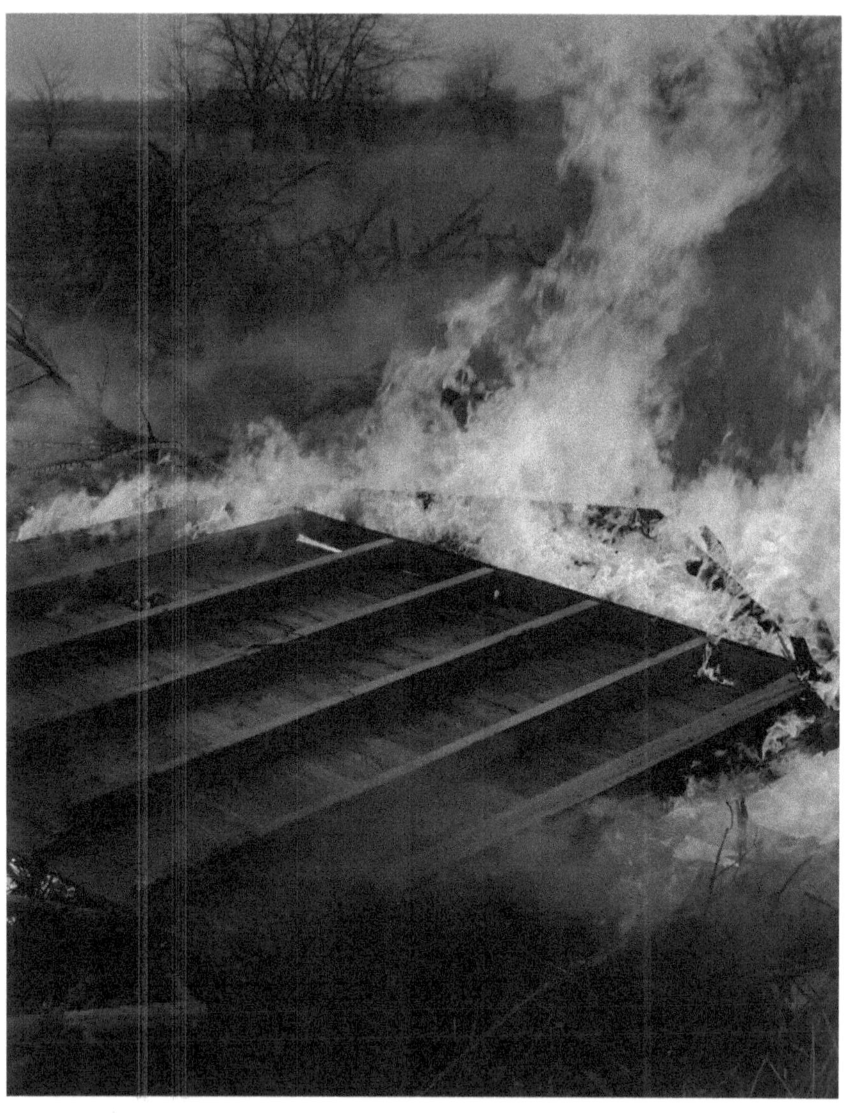

Recollect #3.

from the west. Into the Fred Meyers parking lot. Out of the Fred Meyers parking lot. Straight south on 148th Circles within circles. Across Powell to the dead-end at an ancillary trail to Powell Butte Nature Park.

Alyssa and Chino: Exit opposite sides of the Escort.

Chino: Gun clip thrown ahead of where they're running, deep into the woods. Woods don't care.

Alyssa and Chino: Uphill. Long, fear-fueled, strides. Instant sobering in the cool night.

[Multiple car doors open and shut after the siblings vanish into trees. Radio static and squelches.]

Reel runs out. Forest keeps going.

Fully Developed

(All combustible materials have been ignited. The hottest, most dangerous, stage of a fire for anyone who is trapped inside.)

Powell Butte Nature Park is an extinct volcanic cinder cone covering a total of 612 acres. Elevation 600 feet. The park is flanked by neighborhoods on the north and west sides, Johnson Creek to the east, the Springwater Corridor bike trail to the south. There are eight different access points onto the butte, some of them transitioning almost immediately from populated residential areas directly onto over nine miles of intersecting trails. The trails meander through cedar forests, grassland plains, over and along numerous creeks. There are random vagrant camps hidden in the brush, scattered blips of hushed party teens comings and goings, and all the nocturnal wildlife the butte has to offer. All watching from, or for, the shadows. All breathing at different rates.

Alyssa and Chino are only a few blocks up Elderberry Trail. Cop cars are piling up at the trailhead around the recently abandoned 1999 Ford Escort. Chino on Alyssa's heels. Darkness in front of them, wayward flashlights behind.

Alyssa initially runs from the driver's seat onto the Elderberry trail. She stays on Elderberry at the bifurcation, her pink converse barely visible, Chino is close behind. Alyssa isn't making conscious choices. It's all based on instinct and her propensity to veer left. The sirens are skidding to stops in the gravel behind them. The utility belts clattering from car seats. Cops saying, "Ugh," and breathing hard.

Arms pumping at her sides like she was back in track, freshman year. Lungs not the same. Legs not the same.

Car doors, who knows how many, continue to open and close in the clearing behind them.

The path before Alyssa, defined enough to navigate, even at night, but thick with roots and unevenness.

Alyssa registers rummaging. Movement. A faint clattering on the Dogwood trail not taken. Some cops take the wrong path, some cops stay straight.

Someone, not a cop saying, "What the hell, man?"

The realization that it isn't just Chino and her and the sirens ending their song out here. There are other humans. Other things. There's been cougar sightings for the last month or so. So, maybe, also that. Also, cougars. Pet cats have gone missing. Telephone poles have been peppered, in neighborhoods surrounding the butte, with warnings and heart-filled pleas to help find Muffy or Muppet or Miffy.

Alyssa turns her head multiple times back to Chino, with her finger bumping against her lips (her legs straining, muscles burning) as a warning to shut the hell up as they flee. Stop breathing so hard. *Throw the change in your pockets into the woods already!* she wants to say but doesn't. Afraid of running right into something that would open its glowing eyes just before attacking. Afraid of jail cells and records mounting in unmusical ways.

There's maybe two hours until sunrise. Two hours with the possibility of glowing eyes emerging from the blessings of concealment and the curses of shadows. Even in darkness the forest has come to life around them. Chirpings and chortles. Creaking and crunching. Flashlight beams bouncing off branches and leaf canopies.

Voices saying, "Stop right there," directed in their general direction and nowhere near them. Cops yelling at ghosts, yelling at trees, yelling at yelling.

Chino hissing, "I can't. I can't." Holding his chest.

"You're just going to stop? Out here?" Alyssa whisper-yelling.

Chino's feet picking up speed.

A voice on the path not taken. "Hey man, what the fuck!" some stoner yells into the night, far away down the Dogwood trail. The scrunching of utility belts battling uphill. The stretching of pants not made to run in. Alyssa once heard that cops carry an extra thirty pounds of gear on them. She hopes that's wrong. She hopes it's so much more.

At the top of the Elderberry trail Alyssa and Chino tee into a path wide enough to drive a car down. No cop cars on it. Yet. There might be gates to open at the far ends, people to call to open them, but this path is too wide to run down for too long. Too much risk and exposure. She turns right towards a set of wooden stairs zigzagging up and out of sight, built into the hillside.

Her legs say, *"No."*

Her nature says, *"No."*

Survival says, *"Shut up and move it!"*

Chino keeps trying to tighten his belt. He's running with one hand holding his pants up and the other arm pumping at his side. Midway up Chino says, "Fuck. This. Shit," but keeps taking stairs until he tops them and crosses Pipeline Lane (called so because of the large-diameter, ribbed pipe paralleling the path). There are headlights and spotlights on the wide-pathed trail behind them at the foot of the stairs. Cops and cop cars defying gravity somewhere below them like a reverse game of Donkey Kong where Donkey Kong throws the barrels from the bottom and they roll *up* the platforms after you and handcuff you and ruin your life.

After running for who-knows-how-long on the small path, Alyssa goes off the trail into the trees and thick ground moss. Chino follows her. There are invisible soft earth holes that eat your leg up to the knee. They push their way over fallen branches. They can't keep running. Need to rest. But not here, not yet.

When they stop, Chino starts picking up the moss and mulch around them and rubbing it on his clothes and face.

"What the fuck, Chino?"

"Scent camouflage, Lis. For the dogs of war."

"Does that really work?"

"Who knows? Can't hurt."

Alyssa bends down and grabs handfuls of earth, rubs them into her cheeks, neck, chest, arms. Bends again. Repeats. Brother and sister mirroring each other in the dark forest. Becoming the dirt and dank of nature.

They hear siren bleeps alternating in all directions. Some further, some closer.

Chino knows what they're doing. This is how cops ferret you out of hiding. Shepherd you into handcuffs. The slipknot approach: a decreasing circumference to strangle you out. It'll be a lot harder for them to do on acreage this big, with so little car access, but they'll try.

"How much can these cops really care about catching us? Asks Alyssa. "A window was shot out. Nobody was hurt." She looks into her moss-covered brother's eyes. "Right? Nobody was hurt?"

"No. I mean, I doubt it."

Alyssa wonders if her brother is lying. She wonders if they can outlast the cops, if they can become something sub-urban, something sub-suburban. It would mean crafty survival and improvised weaponry. Becoming one with the forest. Eating berries. Drinking from streams for as long as it takes, *Lord of the Flies*-style. The more moss that crumbles off Alyssa's clothes, the further she feels herself falling from civilization. It isn't a bad feeling, more of a weightlessness than a falling. Her pink shoes are camouflage. Not pink camouflage, dirt camouflage. She can feel the forest on her, opening a view into her. She smells the dirt and bark and detritus, an immediacy that she can't remember ever feeling before, a power under all the aching and living and fresh scrapes and bruises of the chase.

Alyssa looks at Chino. There are twigs in his disheveled hair, grime on his cheeks, smudges around his forming smile. The smile is the Chino of her childhood. The Chino before the anger and the school fights and the disillusionment. A smile that is uncertain but enchanting.

"Bummy chic?" Chino grins.

"Bummy chic." Alyssa says.

And just as fast as she feels a surge of joy, the joy is dampened by the yelling and sirens bleeping and bushes shaking in the near distance. She pushes all the sound back and feels the smile coming back over her. Alyssa knows that this is how they stay alive and free out here: their ability to adapt to anything. Their ability to laugh through anything. The ease in which they remember the dirt. Their skills at becoming their surroundings. The corners of her eyes lose their tension.

And that's when she notices the two glowing spheres just over Chino's shoulder. Two moons. Not two moons.

Her confidence leaves her body in one stilted exhale.

"Chino," she whispers, "Walk slowly to me."

"What is it?"

"There's eyes."

"Oh shit, fuzz?"

"No." Alyssa's eyes don't blink. "Wild ones."

You're not supposed to run from a predator, somebody had once said that at some point. Alyssa remembers someone saying not to bend down or make yourself look smaller. She should have picked up a stick or branch before now. But what would a stick do against those eyes?

She breathes in little, short breaths.

She is not the dirt. She is not the night. Those eyes are the night. Bright and insane. A hiss below the night eyes. A cougar? A raccoon? A possum? All the moss trembling off Chino as he spins toward the sound, probably faster than he should, pushing his back to Alyssa's chest, arms extended out to his sides to appear bigger. "Let's discuss the implications of one hissing at another in the night," Chino says, always trying to say something stupid before he's in way over his head. Already in over his head. Words don't work like that out here. Or do they?

The four-legged shadow body behind the eyes, postures. There is a rustle of bushes, a blur of brown, two bodies landing with a bone crunch in the underbrush. A struggle. A bigger crunch.

Alyssa doesn't believe in things happening so quickly. But things are happening everywhere, always, life spinning in and out of existence without malice or kindness. Always survival is happening. Always something is dying or being born.

On the forest floor, in front of the siblings, a cougar stands over a raccoon's twitching body. The cougar considers Chino, glimpses at Alyssa. Chops-licking. Stance-readying. Alyssa doesn't know if she's ever been so afraid of something so beautiful. Every muscle of the cat tenses with purpose. Every movement has a rhythm. When everything slows down and the radio static in her ears is indistinguishable from the ocean, when an under-growl is the only the sound of the unknown beckoning a beyond, something inside you either opens or collapses.

Chino backs slowly against Alyssa. His back to her chest. Alyssa backs away slowly. Her chest to his back. They almost stumble over fallen trees and barrier ferns, but they don't. They find rhythm. They take it slow-slow. They make themselves bigger as they fade into darkness. The cougar watching. The cougar calculating. The cougar waiting, without moving, for the two strange dirt creatures to exit the stage.

Decay

(A significant decrease in oxygen, fuel, or heat that eventually leads to the fire's extinguishment.)

Alyssa and Chino travel as far as they can within the dense forest area between trails. They are silent. Their ears are honed to the vibrations around them. When they can't walk anymore, they lie down on the forest floor. The pinecones and needles. The sun is beginning to reach into the sky. All the cortisol and adrenaline has been burned up in their bodies. The forest noises

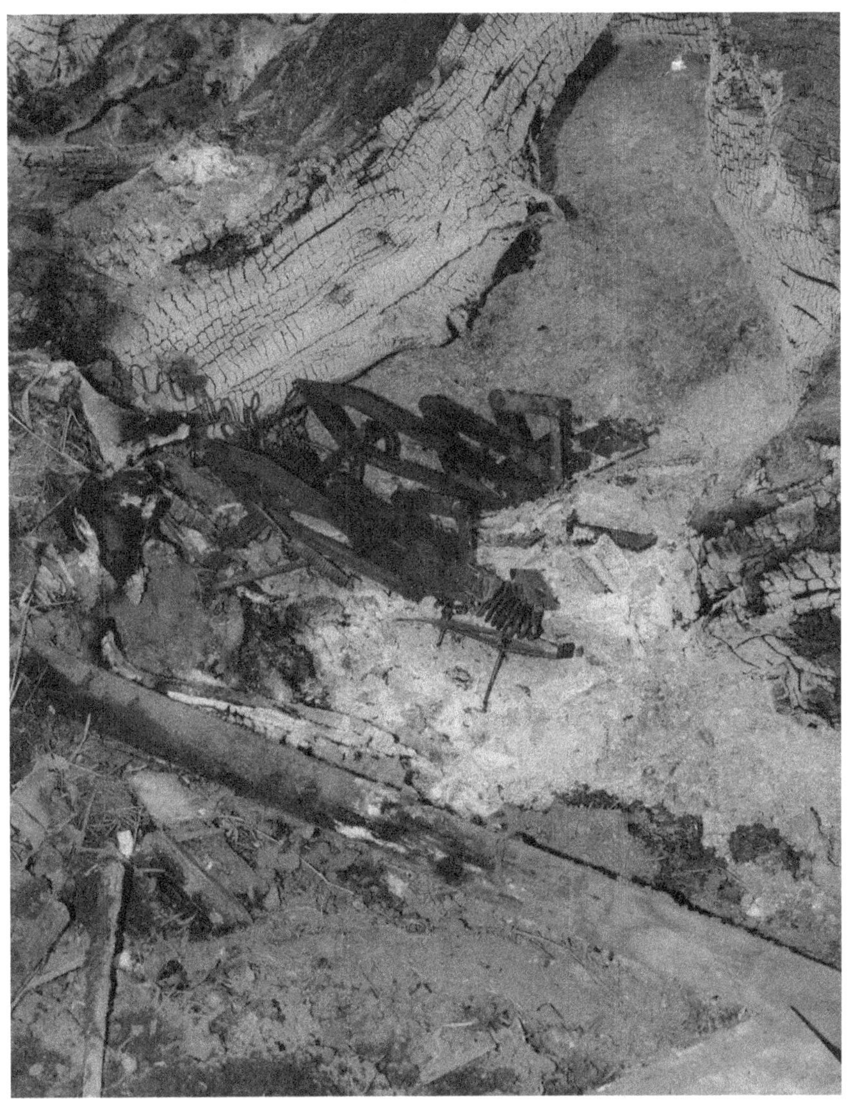

Recollect #4.

are only an organic wave machine app turned on around them. The squelches and siren blips are only the presence of one of their mother's parties from when they were younger, still going on the other side of the bedroom wall they shared as children. The ground is a horrible bed, but a welcomed rest.

"I'm sorry," says Chino.

"Yeah."

"I am."

"I know. They'll know it's your car, though."

"I know."

Alyssa doesn't mean to fall asleep but, somehow, she does. She dreams of a cougar stalking her across an expanse of ice. The ice never ends, cold-white forever. She feels like the cougar is toying with her. Sometimes the ice camp she erects shows signs that the cougar's been there while she slept. A freshly dead rabbit for a meal. Three whiskers left outside her tent. A fresh pile of scat by the wispy coals. Within the dream, she starts to wonder if the cougar wants to harm her or help her. Maybe the cougar is still deciding the same.

When Alyssa awakens all her muscles are sore. She's been drooling on her bicep. It's light out. There's no telling how late or how early it is. The squelching and the sirens are either gone or lying-in wait. Alyssa ambles her way through the roughage to the nearest trail with Chino on her heels. Once on the trail they brush themselves off as much as possible, bat at each other's backs, muss each other's hair. There are no cops here.

They still don't have words for each other. Alyssa and Chino walk down the backside of Powell Butte via the Hawthorne trail. Through the tall grass to Cedar Grove trail. Along the paved path to the Springwater Corridor. There are no cops here.

They walk the corridor east and turn left on 172nd Street, unembarrassed of the smudges and grime still clinging to them.

They turn left on Stark Street.

This is how street people must feel, like soldiers coming back from war, still at war.

They walk to their mother's apartment and half mile west. It's the longest walk home either of them has ever taken. When they turn into the parking lot of the complex the cop cars are here. They resign to stop running. When they open the door their mother rushes to embrace them.

Alyssa and Chino sit on the living room sofa with one cop standing over them and one cop on the edge of the recliner at their side. Their mother is standing next to the kitchen worrying her fingers over each other.

"So, your car was stolen last night, and the assailants kicked the two of you out in *some woods on the way to Mt. Hood*? One was *a skinny white guy* and the other was *a fat white guy*? You didn't call anybody because you *didn't have service* and eventually your *phones died*?" says the standing cop, making finger quotations while he reads Chino's actual words back to him. "Does that sound right?"

"Yes sir," says Chino.

"Okay, makes sense." The cop adjusts his utility belt, scratches at his head.

"So, was that before or after you shot the Plaid Pantry window out?" He taps his pen against his bottom lip. "Come on, Chino. You're not an idiot. You've got to know there's cameras everywhere."

"That was," starts Chino. "Yeah, okay, I guess I need a lawyer." Chino's words running out of options. "She had nothing to do with it, though. I made her go along."

"Let's talk about where you got the gun from. And where it is now."

Salvage & Overhaul

(After a structure fire is out, the walls and ceilings are opened with hand tools to check for fire extension into the voids and in between spaces. If not done properly the hidden embers will start fires of their own.)

Their mother worries with her hands, one over the other, while Chino is placed in cuffs. She worries her hands at his trial. She worries her hands every time she is in the visitor area of the prison in Salem, every time she thinks about his future, every time Alyssa is late coming home.

Alyssa gets community service and later enrolls in community college and takes classes that are interesting and eye-opening.

Her mother says, "Your open eyes aren't going to pay the bills."

"Maybe though," Alyssa says. "Maybe."

She gets a job at a mall clothing store, takes her classes at night.

In one of the letters Alyssa writes to Chino she tells him how Powell Butte was once land to the Tribes of the Grand Ronde. She sends pictures of all the other mountains you can see from the top of the butte. She visits the other buttes within the same extinct volcano chain. They are within a couple miles of each other. She'd never known about them before. Alyssa asks Chino, in her letters, if he's been having dreams of cougars since their night on the butte. She tells him that they recently killed a cougar on the Elderberry trail. She doesn't know exactly who *they* are. She writes, *I hope it wasn't our cougar.* She writes, *cats are still going missing*. She writes, *isn't a cougar a cat, too?*

Alyssa is uncertain about her future and her family and all the paths leading from here to forever. But when she closes her eyes in the forest and stays very still, she can see embers glimmering inside her. She feels the wind moving through her. She hears her heart beating around her. There is a growl in the sky, a spark on the horizon, a rekindling within.

ALONZO WAS A WELDER

Words: Rich Perin

Art: Daniel Crayonton

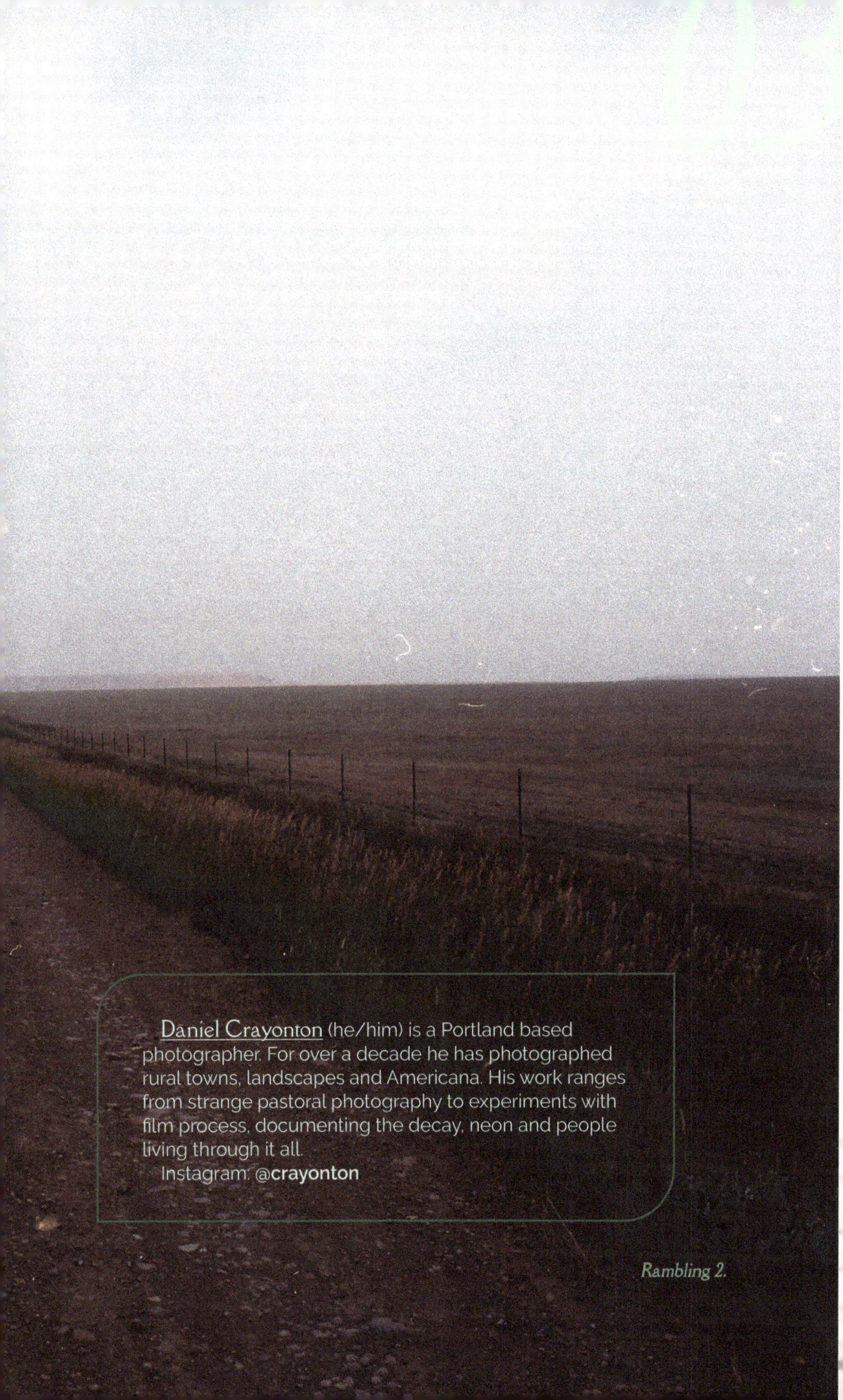

Daniel Crayonton (he/him) is a Portland based photographer. For over a decade he has photographed rural towns, landscapes and Americana. His work ranges from strange pastoral photography to experiments with film process, documenting the decay, neon and people living through it all.

Instagram: @**crayonton**

I need a little extra cash to see myself through while I lay low, so I call Dylan de Biers. He's currently in Melbourne, Australia, renting eight rooms in an old hotel above a pub. It's noon his time.

"Hello?"

"Dylan, it's me."

"Oh, hello! What do you know? Rich-hard! Is that really you?" He is over-emphasizing his diction like a thespian. "I was just saying to Bree the other week that we haven't heard from Rich-hard in a long time and he never returns our calls. Bree! Guess who has graced us? Yes, it's really him! We should sacrifice a calf!"

"Yeah, yeah, yeah, sorry," I say. "I got your messages. I should have called earlier but you know how it is."

"Not really. But I am familiar with you," Dylan says, returning to his natural voice. "Where are you?"

"On the interstate, cutting through Idaho, heading to the farm." The coupe is riding 5 mph above the speed limit. The Sawtooth Mountains are fading in the rear mirror, the Blue Mountains of eastern Oregon hunched ahead.

"I'm not going to ask where you're fleeing from."

I correct him. "Man, I never flee. Assholes flee. I always depart in good grace."

"It's easy to hang around too long and not realize you've hung around too long," responds Dylan.

"Not with me, buddy." I change the subject. I don't really want to talk about where and what I've done for the last year. "How are you? And Bree?"

"Good. Good. Yes, good. She's making dinner tonight, even Pavlova for dessert, going all out like a chef. Roast lamb with mint sauce. Have you ever tried that?" Dylan was never into refined dining. Food was an expenditure, and he was thin. Ground beef and caviar were not that discernable to his tastes, the difference he noticed most was price.

"I think the last time I had roast lamb was in Australia," I say. "Maybe ten years ago. You and the lady celebrating?"

"Not really. Bree's into cooking at the moment." says Dylan. "We do have news, though. Haven't really told anyone, don't want to jinx it."

I joke, "Bree's pregnant."

There's a pause. I can't hear Dylan breathing. Maybe the call dropped. Then Dylan breaks the silence. "Why... yes. How did you know?"

"Seriously?"

"Yes. In six months, if things go according to plan."

"Wow."

"I know, right?"

I feel like laughing but recognize that isn't right. I respond with customary pleasantry instead. "Congratulations! That's great news. How's Bree?"

"Absolutely radiant."

"She always was."

"Well, yeah, but even more radiant. She has a luminosity. Wait a minute," Dylan moves the phone away from his mouth and yells, "Hey Bree, what about Luminosity as a name for the baby? No? Yeah, you're right. On second thought it does sound dodgy."

I have trouble believing the news. Dylan is only two years old than me. He's rounding up to 50. "You're joking, right?"

"No. Luminosity is a horrible name." Dylan pauses for me to react. He

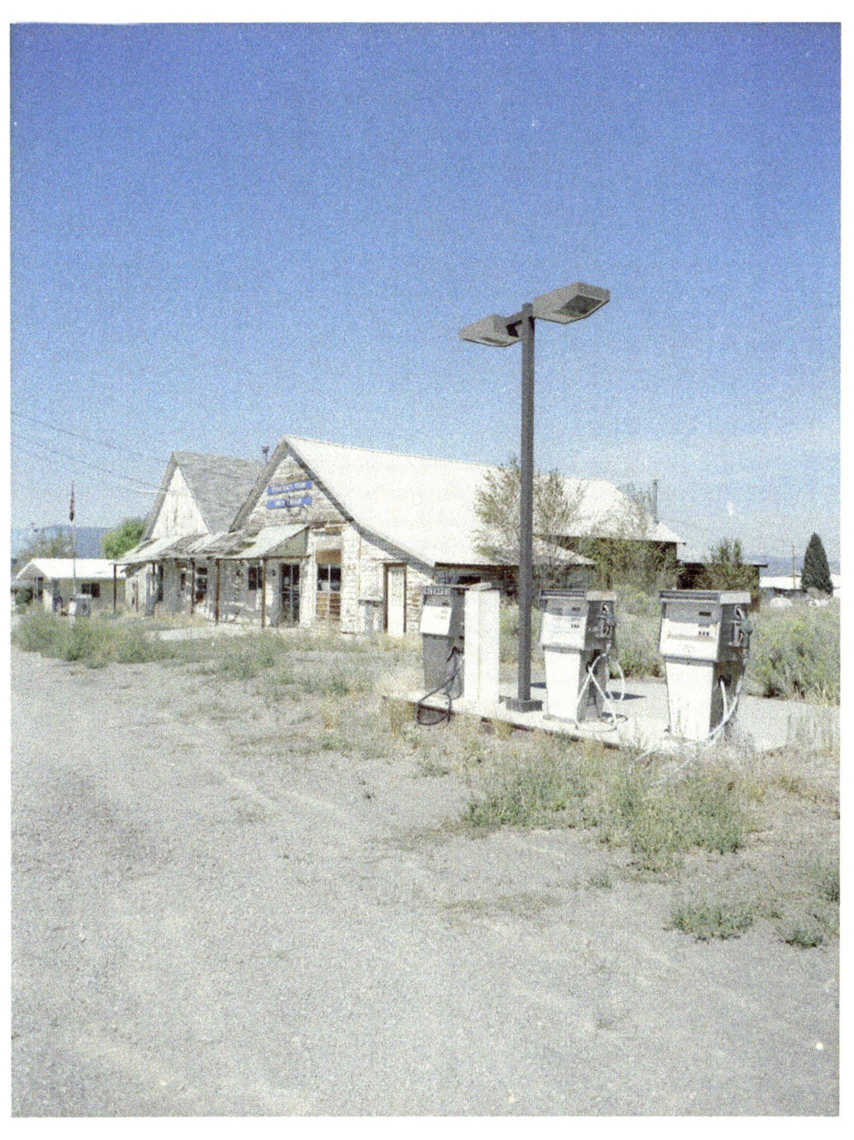

Rambling 3.

doesn't get a reaction. Then, "I know it sounds like a joke. Me, a father. But yes, I can confirm the biology works. My sperm still swim strong."

"Wow. Hot damn, buddy. Congratulations. More power to you."

The tone of Dylan's voice loses animation. "Maybe I am a little old for this," he says. "But I don't feel old. I dye my hair, and no one notices. Besides Bree. She wants to dye it blonde." Maintaining his shoulder-length hair jet black, along with his thin frame, Dylan retains the impression of a thirty-something, and in the right light, maybe even younger. Youth drains from his face much more slowly than his contemporaries. He still has that lost look of someone who just graduated college. Many fell for it, then realized much later that it was only a look. "I know I've never really thought about being a father, someone calling me Dad. Never planned on being one. But the more I think about it, I know what *not* to do. Besides, Bree is the best. I'll just follow her lead."

"That's a good rule of thumb for you."

"Ha! Yes, yes, yes," he mumbles into silence. "And you, what is happening with you?"

"I'm going to need some money. I thought you could provide me with suggestions."

"What are you thinking?"

"I'm willing to place a bet on anything, just as long it's the right bet." Dylan de Biers, 49 years old, had never been employed, nor ever searched for employment. Trying his luck at various money schemes was more interesting than working for someone else. He started in high school, trading musical equipment, then trading very-used-cars, then to whatever he thought he could buy and turn a profit. The margins were skinny but enough to make a living, although Dylan's standard of living was never high. Still, he earned enough to remain unemployed and, instead, pursue his love of music at his convenience. He managed to attain a healthy following in Berlin, Germany, leading a band playing, what he terms, *sonic goth*. In the last decade, though, he tired of the scene, the luster of the of gigs rusted, and he turned to operating short-term rentals in Berlin which provided a reliable flow of income. Whenever he needed larger amounts of money, like his real estate ventures, he delved into the world of internet gambling. Dylan didn't bet often, but when he did the bets were large. What gives him the edge, he says, is his study of biorhythms, something he fell into during high school and discretely practiced ever since. Discretely because he knew people thought poorly of it and, more so, for those that practiced it.

"What about elections?" asks de Biers. "Getting the candidates' birthdates and other astrological data is easy."

The mathematical world of biorhythms. Birthdate, time of birth, dates of significant life events, give them to Dylan de Biers and he'll return a number of numbers reflecting physical, emotional, and intellectual powers. When the three powers rise at the same time, that's a winner. Dylan lived on the proceeds of Barack Obama winning the 2008 election for almost a decade. He placed the bet for Obama to win 18 months in advance, declaring that he had never seen such unified and high numbers as those for Obama.

"I have no stomach for politics at the moment," I respond.

"So what? This is gambling. I'd place bets on Putin."

"Trump took the fun out of it. I'll bet on anything else. What about tennis?

There's always a world invitational going on somewhere."

"Athens Open starts in a few days."

"Bingo. I'll wager on that."

"I'll run the dates and let you know who'll win," says Dylan. "Can I contact you at this number?"

"No. Call the farm number."

"When was the last time you were there?"

"Over a year. Too long. I don't know why I leave it. I am at my best sitting in a rocking chair on a porch watching the greenery, floating in peace and serenity."

"You don't need money straight away, do you? The rhythms maybe out of phase for a while. As your financial advisor I suggest you wait until the waves align."

"No problem, I can wait. I just finished being a real estate agent."

"I thought selling a mansion or two would set you up good."

"My last sale was helping a young couple buy their first home. They thought they couldn't afford but I got them a steal."

"You should do that for me and Bree."

"I said young couple. You folks are a May-December thing."

Dylan laughs.

"Seriously though," I continue, "how's you? You got enough money?"

"Oh yeah, yeah. There's never enough of it but we have enough. I never used to worry too much about money but with a kid on the way, well, I'll adapt. Besides, the government gives you money for having children."

"That's a whole new angle for you."

"Yes. Exactly. I'd be foolish not to take advantage of it."

"Makes me wonder why you didn't have kids earlier."

"Ha! I know! My kid is going to learn some odd things from me. I wouldn't be able to do this with any other woman. The kid would end up too weird."

"Well, that's a realization. You sound happy. I guess you won't be paying a visit stateside anytime soon."

"No, I am going to have to learn new ropes. Look, I have to tell you something."

"You're going to name the child after me?"

"No. We're hoping for a girl."

"Richenda?"

"What?"

"Richenda is the female form of my name. It's Rich with an enda, which is like an Edna."

"No, no. This is something else."

"Okay."

Dylan's voice returns to the less animated seriousness. "Have you ever thought that you may have a kid out in the world?"

"Not really. I just figure my sperm aren't great swimmers like yours. I dated Amelia for three years and there was never a scare. Why? Do you think you have a kid out there already?"

"I've never really thought about that." He pauses, the silence of pondering. "Shit. I suppose there's a chance a little de Biers is out there already. Maybe more than one."

"What makes you think that?"

"No. Wait. Let me explain. I'm getting side-tracked. I'll start again. I got

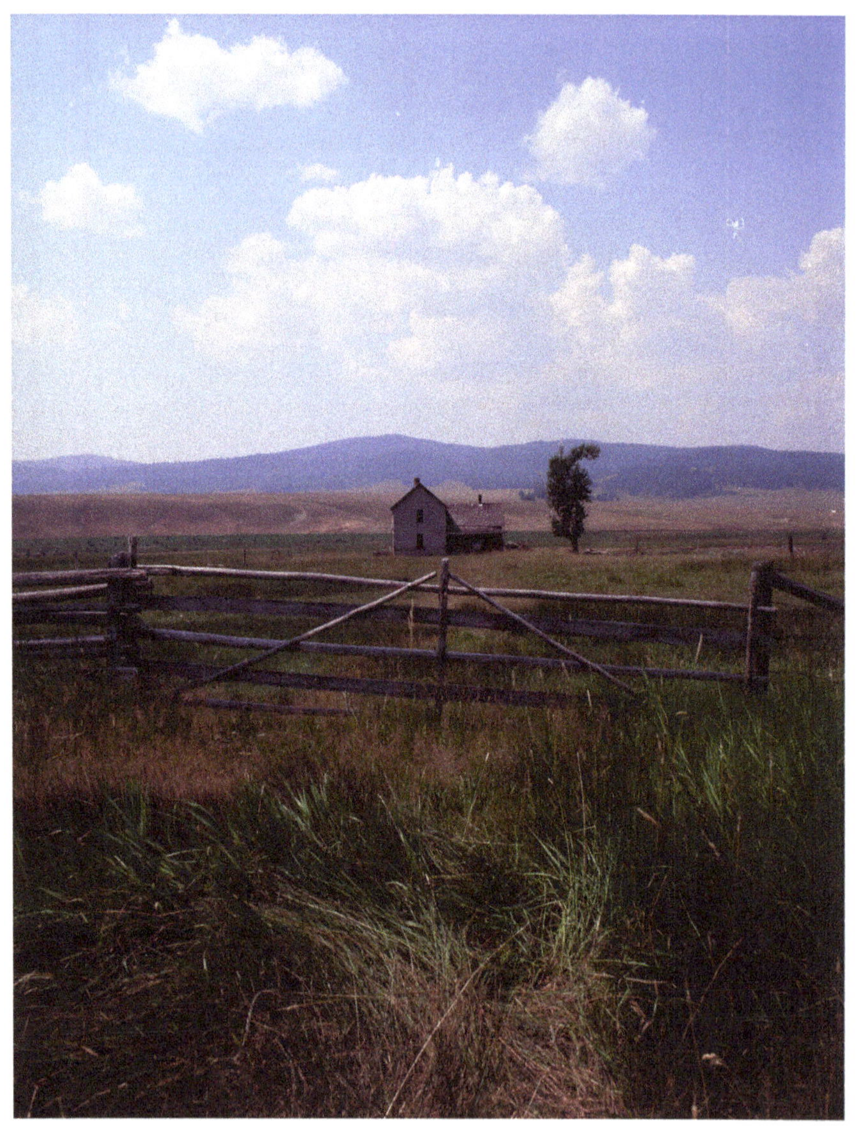

Rambling I.

a phone call the other day. About three weeks ago. It was from America. I wrote her name down. Where is it? I'm trying to find it now." I hear shuffling of papers, things falling to the floor, on his end of the line. "I remember her first name. Adair. I thought that's an interesting name, so I can remember that. Adair. And then her surname was something Mexican. Where is that piece of paper? Do you know her? Adair. Adair Cortez. Something like that."

"Can't say it sounds familiar."

"Adair Cortez? Are you sure?"

"What is this about? Saying Adair Cortez, a bunch of times doesn't ring any familiarity. Is she someone you knew from Berlin?"

"No, no. I've never met her. She's from Texas."

"Haven't set foot in that state since 2012."

"From Austin."

"I left Austin back in 2000."

"She was looking for someone called Alonzo Devas Lolocanzo. She says Alonzo used to be a welder."

"Hey, that was my name in Austin. When I was a welder."

"I know," says Dylan. "There's more. She said that Alonzo might not be his real name. She said he also goes by Rich Perin."

This surprised me. Not many knew my real name. "How the fuck did she find that out. What did you say?"

"I told her I never heard of Dick Previn. Or Alonzo."

"Did she believe you?"

"I don't know. Worrying about if she believes me invites suspicion, don't you think? Well, that's how it works with me. She was on the phone on the other side of the planet so she couldn't read my face. I told her firmly. I didn't stutter."

"I haven't weld in years," I say. "Not since Austin. Decades ago." It was a passing fancy, a random encounter, an impulse buy. In a convenience store parking lot, on Riverside Drive, a guy I never saw before selling from the back of his truck a blow torch, gas tank, gloves, and mask for something like 50 bucks. Seemed like a good skill to learn, an industry accustomed to payment under the table. I practiced learning the basics late at night, just beyond the east end of Town Lake, torching various metals and practicing welds. The power of the flame, it's roar and holy glow, got my attention. There's always work for welders, even substandard ones. Some of my early welds were messy, but I always believed structurally sound. This phone call from Texas, though, made me think otherwise, maybe my welds were hinky, one of my junctions failed, and authorities are tracking down the welder responsible. I ask Dylan, "Did the woman say what state agency she was from?"

"No, no, nothing like that. She was young. Like 20."

"What do you mean? She's not a woman because she's 20?"

"Hang on. I'm messing this up," then the sound of a hand over a phone, a mumbled conversation, the back and forth getting shorter and curter. A rustling of a contested hand-off.

"Hello, Rich, how are you?" It's Bree. She's more than a dozen years younger than Dylan. She's charming, elegant, inquisitive. On the face of it, she and Dylan are a poor match, but somewhere deep their roots tangle and together they flourish.

"Good to hear your voice, Bree. I understand congratulations are in order."

"Yes, thank you. I never thought about becoming a mother but for some reason everything is clicking. I'm keen." Her voice quickly loses levity. "Look, that woman that called from Texas? Her name is Adair Castro. She says she's your daughter."

"What?"

"You have a daughter in Texas, and she is looking for you."

"No, I don't."

"Just because you think you don't doesn't mean you don't."

"How did this happen?"

"You need to deal with this," insists Bree. "There's responsibilities when you have a child."

"Jaysus, I don't have a child."

"She says she's your daughter and I tend to believe her. Okay. Dylan is flapping his arms about and scowling at me. I'll put him back on the phone and you two can work it out, probably too slowly." More muffling and ruffling.

"Rich, you still there?" asks Dylan. "Rich? Hello?"

"I'm here. Let's start this again. Slowly. Don't leave anything out."

Dylan begins. "Last Wednesday, I get a phone call. A young woman introduces herself. Adair..." and I can hear Bree in background whispering *Castro*, which Dylan repeats, "Castro. That's right. Adair Castro. She's got a yank accent and asks to speak to Dylan de Biers. I say that's me. I got that five-year visa and I thought it might be the yanks checking up, important to stay on the government's good side. So, I say, yes, that's me. Then she tells me her name, a short bio, she's from Austin, twenty years old, her mother just passed away, and she was trying to find her father. Alonzo Devas. A welder, who used to live in Austin twenty years ago. She asked if I knew him. I said no. Then she said that he also went by Rich Perin. And I said, no, I do not know any of those names. Then I asked why she called me, and she said that I bought a car, a minivan, from Alonzo twenty years ago, in Austin. I feigned a false, weak recollection about the minivan, saying I thought I bought it at a used car lot. She seemed satisfied with the answer."

"Did she say her mother's name?"

"Yes. What was it? Something like Angela."

"Angelique," I say. "It's Angelique."

"Yes! That's it. Angelique Castro, that's her mother's name."

A name I hadn't recounted in a-whiles. We met at La La's Little Nugget; a dimly lit dive decked in Christmas lights operated by two elderly sisters who appreciated generous pours. Angelique and I easily fell into conversation, I bought her a drink, discovered we enjoyed each other's wit, drank, and laughed some more. An instant connection tuned in the same frequency. That summer we were inseparable, roaming central Texas, a trip to New Orleans, great fun, and freedom until she said it was time to get back to her studies and focus all energies there. Which was fine, the climes of Texas had worn thin with me, and I certainly didn't want to hold her back. "Jaysus. Angelique," I say to Dylan. "Incredibly smart. I felt like I couldn't keep up with her. This was some time ago."

"Well, it only takes one time, no matter how long ago."

"And it's her daughter, this gal that called, says I'm her father?"

"Yeah, she's certain about that," says Dylan. "Adair Castro. So, do you think it's true?"

"This is from left field," I say. "Beyond left field. Zoomed in and hits me right between the eyes." I calculate the years, and the age of Angelique's daughter times right. It's impressive that she found my real name. "Did she leave a contact number or anything."

"Yes. And her email. What are you going to do?"

"I don't know. I need to get to the farm and unpack all this."

"That's just it. It's good you called. She said she is going to Oregon. She has an address. So, don't be surprised to see her when you drive up to the gate. Or play dumb then act surprised. I don't know. It depends on how you want to play it, I guess."

"Wait. She's going to be where now?"

"At the farm. She said she's taking a Greyhound."

I pull the coupe to the side of the highway.

"I didn't even realize that Greyhound buses are still a thing," continues Dylan. "It's a younger person's form of transport. Once I could sleep on anything, anywhere, anytime. But those Greyhound seats, they'd misalign my back now and I'd walk crooked for weeks. The resilience of youth, eh?"

HOW TO GET FREE

Words: Caitlin Delohery Art: Tomás Oliveras

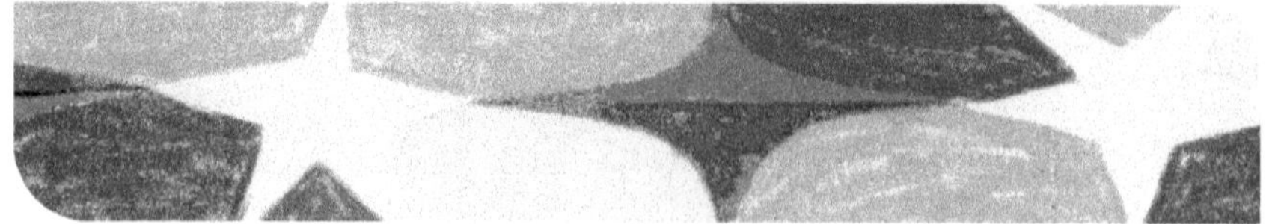

Caitlin Delohery (she/her) is a writer and artist from Portland, Oregon. Her work has been published in the anthology *Indelible in the Hippocampus: Writings on the Me Too Movement* (McSweeney's, 2019), and she's also been featured in *Weird Sister, Lumina, Storyscape*, and other journals. She's a MacDowell Fellow ('09, '19). Her quarantine obsessions have included graphic novels, Tara Brach, Duolingo, baby sheep, and death.

Tomás Oliveras (he/they/she) is a 30 year old QPOC illustrator working primarily in marker portraits and mini polymer clay sculptures. As a self-taught artist, his work reflects the controlled chaos of his methods of creation, straying heavily from traditional portraiture into the world of the surreal. Each piece is created with the intention to both soothe and disturb their viewers. Given their obsession with body language and emotions, Tomás has found himself fixated on capturing the extremity of gaze; leaving their consumers wondering, what the hell are they staring at?

Instagram: **@tomatosita**
Youtube: **Tomasita Rodriguez**
Tiktok: **@tomatosita**

Once upon a time, there was a girl. Or at least, that's what her parents called her at the beginning: *girl*.

She didn't know herself as a girl or as not a girl. She knew herself as something else they didn't have a name for yet, something that didn't need naming. Her parents kept arguing about the name for her, they made charts and pro and con lists, and even talked to a branding agency about it.

None of this mattered to her. What was important, the girl who wasn't a girl thought, was this feeling between her legs. It was like if Santa could sneeze down your chimney. It was like if horses could ride you instead. It was like if you could be inside of a flower the very first time it shivered open to the sun.

Her parents noticed her hungers. It was dangerous, they knew. Someone the world thought of as a girl shouldn't be so hungry. They corseted her unnamed body the way you board up windows before a storm. They hired tutors to teach her how to hold her breath. They took her to the finest doctors, paid for the latest surgeries to make her hungers smaller, to teacup her needs.

She made a bow of her corset strings, arrows with the boning. She threw parties with the art school punks and told her parents stories about packs of wolves destroying the drawing room, drinking up their Pernod, knocking over grandpa's urn and snow angeling in his ashes.

We're just thinking of your future, they said, drawing up plans for a turret to lock her away in. As though her future were a place they would all going together.

They hired police psychics and news forecasters, marketing trend masters and predictive scientists. They mired themselves in facts and data as the sun set in pretty oranges and livid reds outside, as a crow dropped dead in the snow, its tiny legs sticking up straight, a child's drawing of two flowers.

The girl who wasn't a girl saw all of this. The girl who wasn't a girl crawled out her bedroom window like she was crawling out of the wrong timeline. Her heart was a hurricane, twin heats of hunger and sadness.

She started living in the woods outside the art school. Her parents still lived on inside her like lapbands.

She tried to get free through fucking, obeying the old flower feelings. She fucked an alligator, she had a threesome with a pair of mongooses, she dabbled in the fallative arts. She collected fucks the way her parents collected data and still all her winds were howling.

She tried to get free through Pernod, through smoke in her lungs, through those plants that made it feel like other plants could talk to you. The scorch of it all mimicked freedom, but she caught on soon enough.

She went to a moon therapist, who told her she'd been in a thruple with her parents in a past life. She let leeches purple her wrists, drawing out the sadness in her blood. She put crystals on her nipples and cried into a hole in the earth. Her parents would've flipped, but everything stayed the same.

So, she set to work. She would turn herself into the pack of wolves, howling out those lonely songs to call back all the lost parts of her. She would invent a language that didn't need a name for what she was.

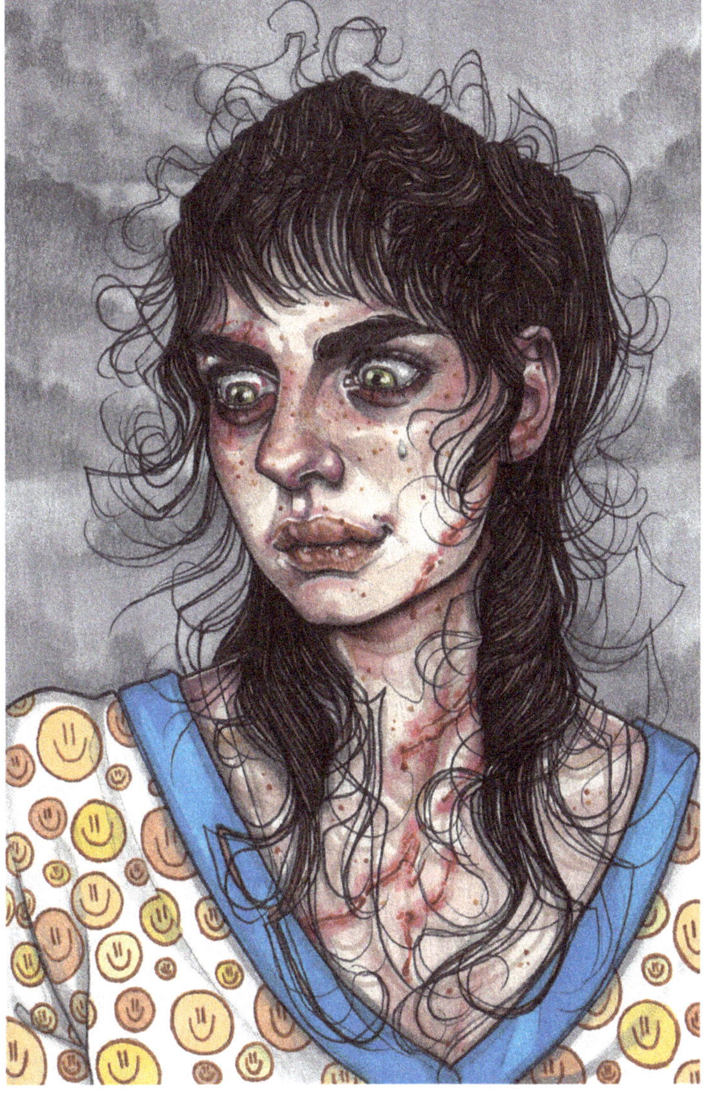

Monolith.

05

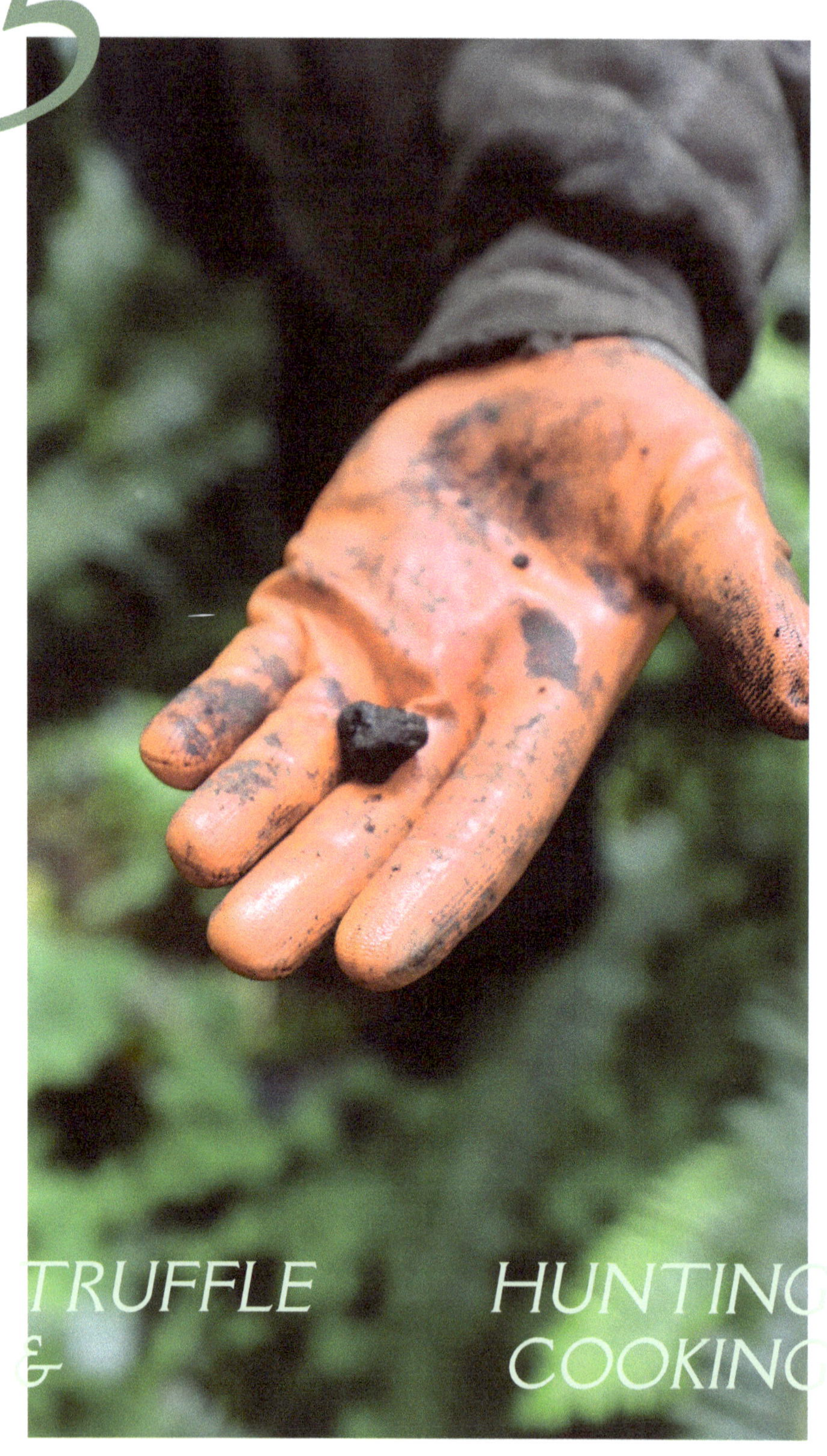

TRUFFLE HUNTING & COOKING

Truffles Are A Type of Fungus. Fungi Are Everywhere And Your Friend

The spectrum of applications fungi covers is astonishing. They give us food, soil, atmosphere, and visions. Molds allow us to make alcohol, bread, cheese, and antibiotics. Then there are the newer fungal revelations, like their powers to consume rock and crude oil, and survive in space. Mycelia, the network below the fruiting bodies of mushrooms, can filter heavy metals and other harmful materials from contaminated water, grow earth-friendly textiles and building materials, while research indicates their antiviral capabilities can protect bees against colony collapse. Their influence is vast but largely subterranean.

Truffles Are The Royalty of Mushrooms

Mushrooms as a food are popular, sure, but still can be polarizing. You may have been served a soggy or slimy brown form and decided you don't like them, or at least know someone who is not interested in eating mushrooms of any kind. The texture is an issue to some. And it is understandable, they can retain a lot of water, as well as absorb whatever liquids or oils or juice they've been cooked in, so unless they are properly seared, roasted, or squeaked (pressing them into the pan with a sturdy spatula as hard as you can), their true culinary glory is easily obscured when incorrectly prepared.

And maybe you have never tried mushrooms beyond white button or Portabella, which are perhaps the least flavorsome varieties. The Pacific Northwest is a fungus paradise, 1,500+ species of mushrooms call their homes here. Coral Tooth, Candy Caps, Shaggy Manes, and Spring Kings are common names of some edible varieties found in Oregon. Arguably one of the most sought-after culinary mushrooms, amongst the apex of the fungal pyramid in terms of not only flavor but price, is the *Leucangium carthusianum*, the Oregon Black Truffle.

Eating an Enigma

Describing the flavor of a truffle is an exercise in ambiguity. Because it is unique and full of subtleties, descriptions often are poetic, trying their best to capture the truffles' glorious funk. They are far more complex than the typical umami of other mushrooms, with notes of cream soda, shallot, and Taleggio. Truffles are somewhat hard, like a root, and best when barely cooked. The only heat they appreciate is when they are grated or super-thinly shaved onto warm food, like a steak or pasta, just before serving. Their flavor can also be infused into just about anything. Oil and butter are common, but because truffles are very aromatic, placing one in a jar of hazelnuts for a few days in the fridge will transform the nut into a decadent treat.

They feel and look like the dirt they came from, damp and a bit drab. But their insides are ornately marbled with cream-colored webbing. Ripe truffles have an earthy scent reminiscent of expensive chocolate laced with the ripest of pineapple. They don't have a long shelf life, and need refrigeration. After a few days, a week at the most, the truffle will smell like rotten garbage.

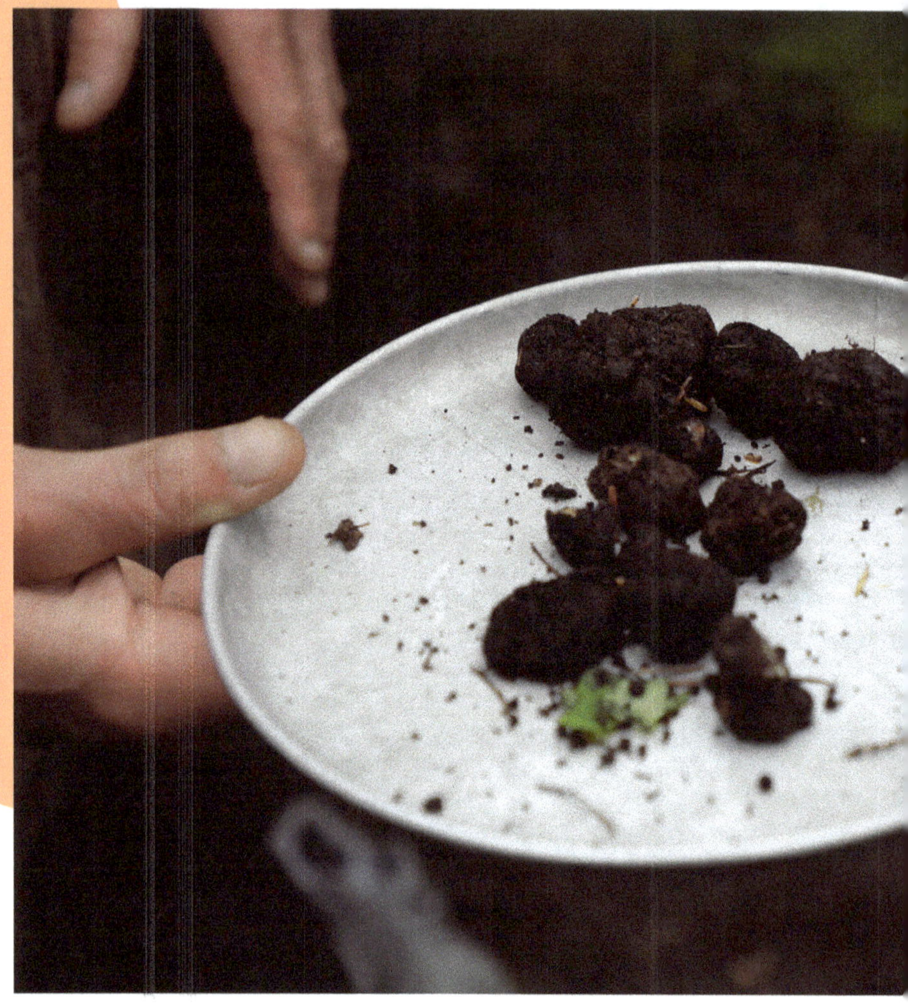

Hunting the Truffle

The Oregon Black Truffle is a wild child and can't be cultivated. Forty minutes outside of Portland, they grow buried a few inches under the forest floor. Once ripe, the truffle lies in fragrant wait. To find them, two things are needed: A dog with a keen snout, and a person who not only knows a place of ideal truffle conditions but is willing to reveal it. Our human guide, Eric, compromised for us, sharing a moderately secret spot (he never reveals his favorite locations), and assured that even though it was late in the season, we wouldn't leave empty-handed. Our canine guide, Doug, knew nothing of the guarantee, but happily obliged. Doug's a decade-old chocolate lab, trained only in the last year as a forager in his backyard after a few sessions of hide and seek, using actual truffles or anything infused with truffle scent as a treasure that earns a treat when found. Eric and Doug's truffle harvest follows minimum intervention. Reckless operators, including some commercial truffles hunters,

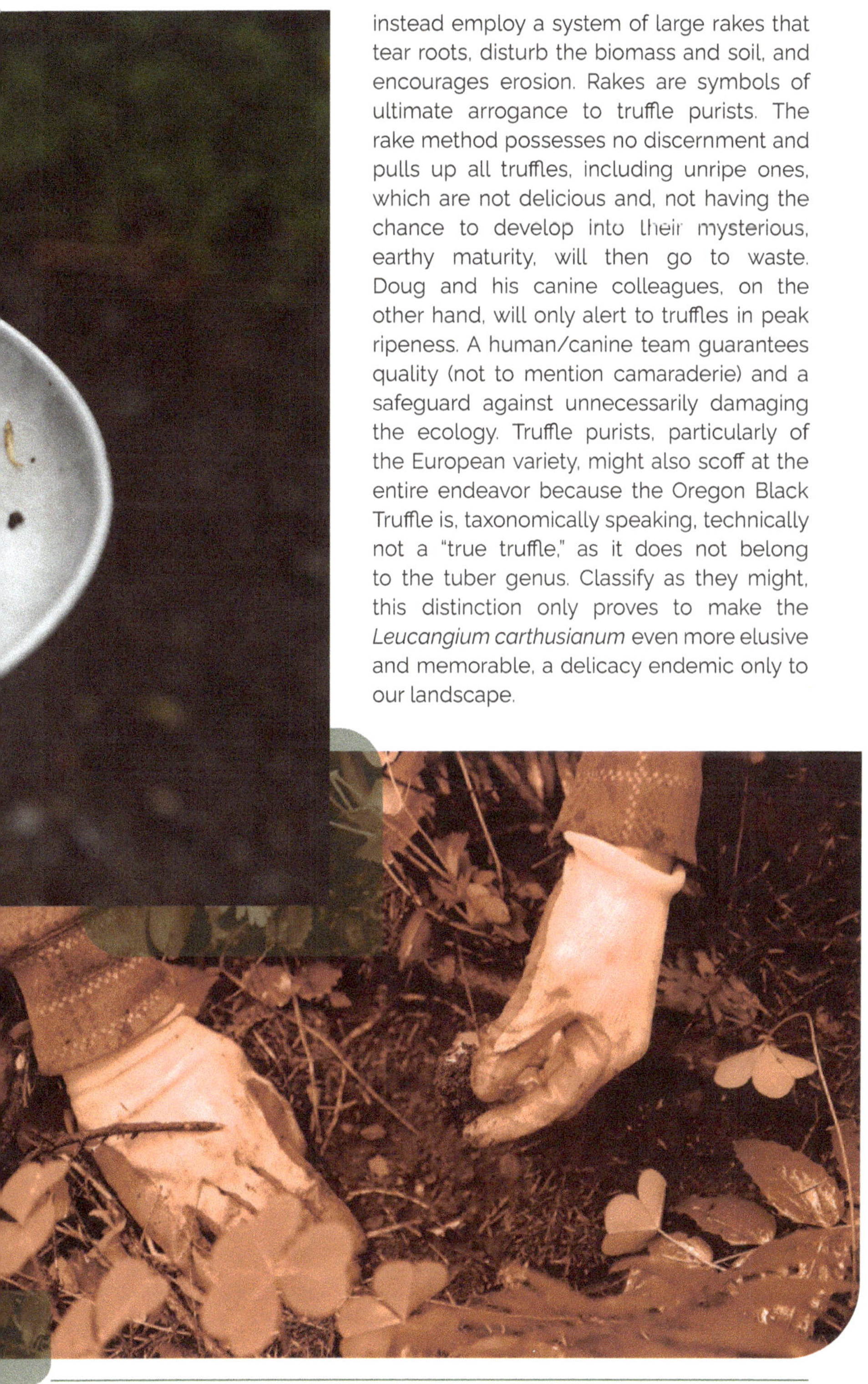

instead employ a system of large rakes that tear roots, disturb the biomass and soil, and encourages erosion. Rakes are symbols of ultimate arrogance to truffle purists. The rake method possesses no discernment and pulls up all truffles, including unripe ones, which are not delicious and, not having the chance to develop into their mysterious, earthy maturity, will then go to waste. Doug and his canine colleagues, on the other hand, will only alert to truffles in peak ripeness. A human/canine team guarantees quality (not to mention camaraderie) and a safeguard against unnecessarily damaging the ecology. Truffle purists, particularly of the European variety, might also scoff at the entire endeavor because the Oregon Black Truffle is, taxonomically speaking, technically not a "true truffle," as it does not belong to the tuber genus. Classify as they might, this distinction only proves to make the *Leucangium carthusianum* even more elusive and memorable, a delicacy endemic only to our landscape.

Doug The Truffler

The location of the hunt seemed like a regular, glorious PNW forest, with sheaths of moss softening the branches, and the air carrying a lush coolness. But for Doug the dog, the scene was far more *beyond*, a realm of intense scent. Lemony Wood Sorrel, aromatic Doug Fir, twitching burrows of mountain beavers below his paws, and a myriad of other verdant forest flooded his nose. The smell sensitivity of dogs is ultra, able to discern and categorize scent like humans do with colors. And so, the singular odor of a ripe black truffle, already dramatic for humans, must be symphonic for Doug.

Eric totes only the essentials: a big spoon for dirt-sifting and collecting the truffle; a container for the bounty; and a stash of quality treats for Doug, in this case, some brisket and queso fresco. The first truffle took only a few minutes of circling to locate, the initial ceremonial whiff rising and locked in, Doug kept the truffles coming after that. Most of them were comparable in size to cherry tomatoes, but some bulged like walnuts with the shell still on. The yield grew until there was enough for a multicourse dinner party. The entire time, all we could do was follow and praise the pup as he plunged his snout into the sword ferns, mouth into the mud, finding truffles just because he could, because we wanted him to, and of course, because the shredded meat and cheese cubes. We settled into it, letting Doug lead the way, then gathering around his signal to unearth the chocolatey orbs. And without fail, each time after the truffle was confirmed, secured from Doug's tongue, his well-earned reward and *good boys* given—the refrain of the day, the immediate next thing said was: "Now, let's go find another."

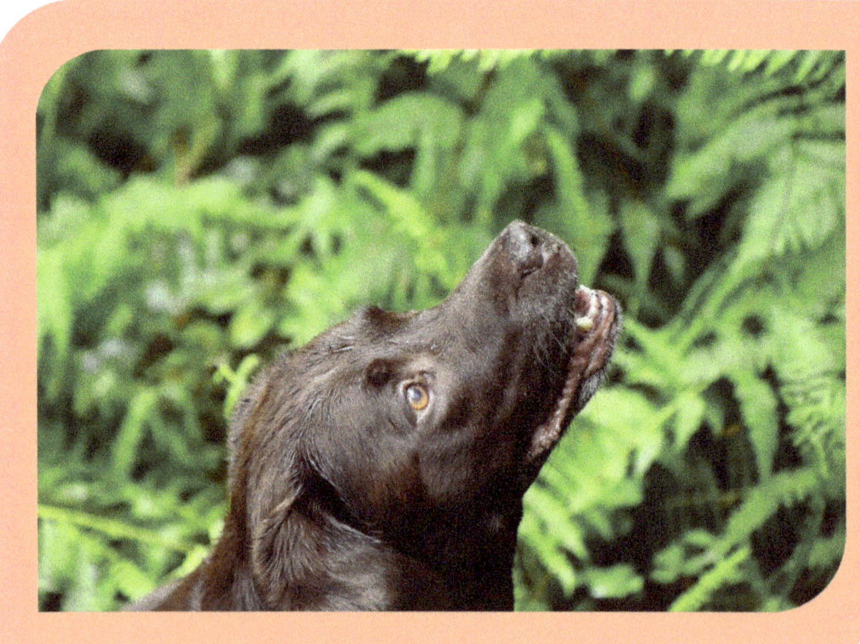

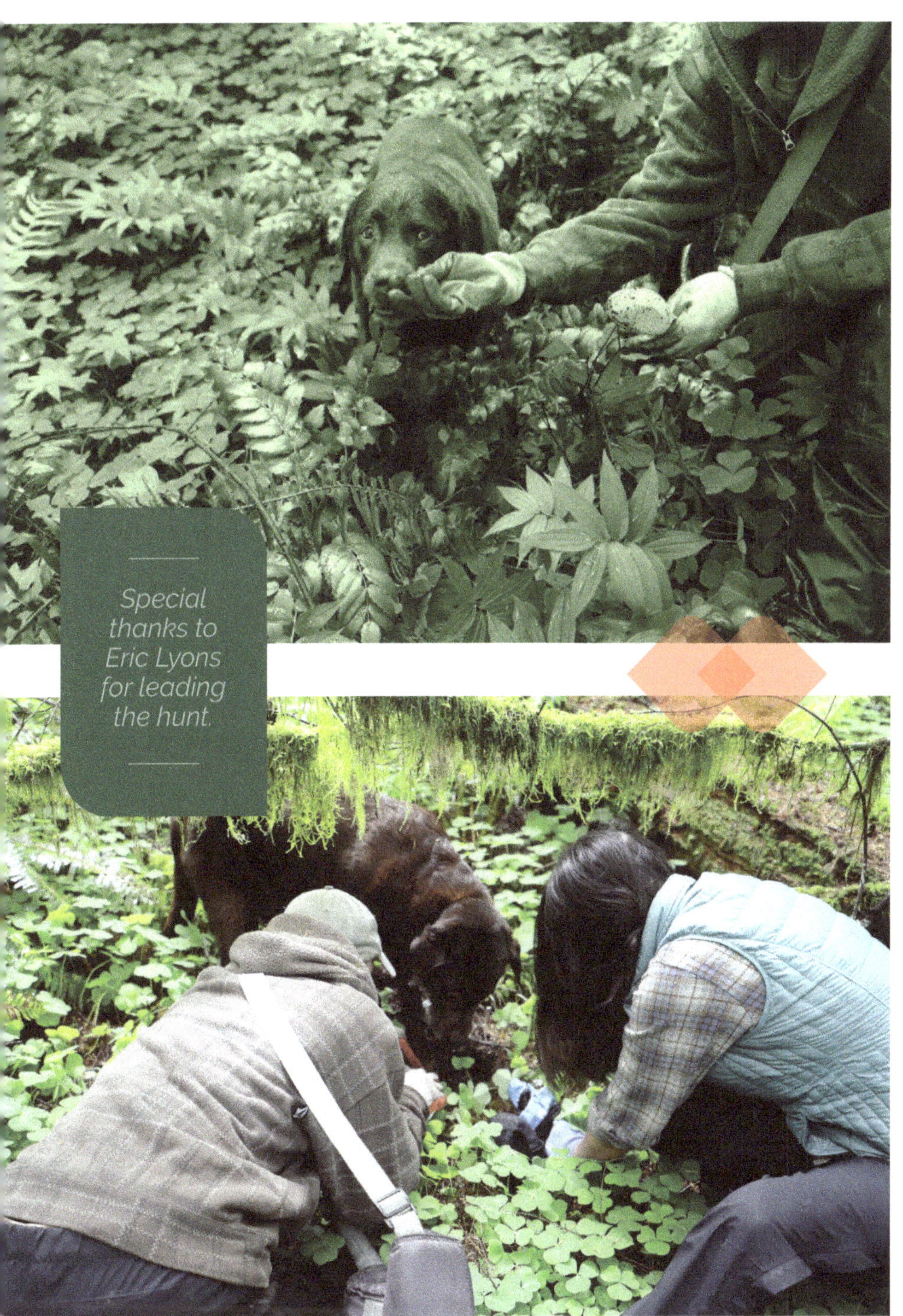

Special thanks to Eric Lyons for leading the hunt.

Old Portland Truffle

Like every other native Portlander I know, I spend too much time lamenting over "old Portland" as if my own youth still exists in some sort of Brigadoon I could stumble back into if I wandered under the bridges late enough, drunk enough, and in a cool enough outfit. But in truth, if Portland snapped back into the shape it was during my glory days as an American Apparel employee, I would likely not be at Rotture's Soul Night or downing countless well gin and tonics at Langano Lounge or even hunkering down in a Beulahland booth for trivia night. Blaming the city for selling out is ultimately easier than admitting I've grown up. But like everyone else, I've spent the past year and a half indoors, getting excruciatingly acquainted with the adult I've become.

After rewatching the entirety of *Buffy* (and *Angel*), implementing a lengthy, multi-stepped skin routine, and investing in a USB powered vibrator, I turned my attention to the roughly one hundred square feet of space in my studio apartment designated as a kitchen. I skipped the sourdough trend, skeptical of my own baking skills, and opted for the more errand-driven work of jamming. I replaced my 9-5 desk job with an all-day project of picking fruit, cooking jam, and jarring my riches. After months quarantined alone, I finally accessed the sense of satisfaction I never could tap into from responding to emails or examining a spreadsheet. I could hold the contents of my day in the palm of my hand.

After all, it was landing a job during the first weeks of Potato Champion's [*a food cart in the Buckman neighborhood*] arrival in 2008 that began my drift from academia to service work. Since then, I've been more able to mark eras of my life according to which dish sink I knew best than any records or movies that were released, the way I wore my hair, and frankly, whoever I dated.

At Potato Champion, I learned to hustle. At Courier Coffee I made life-long friends. The Woodsman Tavern indoctrinated me to family meals and shift drinks. At Han Oak I became part of a family. I left Portland for a three-year stint in L.A. where I mostly learned how easy I had it in Portland, but where I also cultivated a patience for high maintenance guests and refined my expression while interacting with movie stars and praying I didn't betray how hard I was stifling my excitement. Jon Hamm, if you're reading this, I still think about you every day.

I returned to the PNW with a sales job, telling myself it would get me out of the service industry, but after being laid off at the beginning of the pandemic, I was dragged back in like a bank robber ready for just one more heist. What I never knew about those "last job" pictures until I left food service for one paltry year is that the thieves always know they'll be tempted back—not because the cache is too good to pass up but because they want to return.

Before vaccination and mass re-openings, I tiptoed into recipe development thanks to connections from my old office job and, after many months of imposter syndrome, am able (on most days) to claim it as my profession. So, when I was invited to truffle forage at the close of the season (with a truffle sniffing Labrador), the offer felt not only like a solidification in the career I'm freshly pursuing but also an admission that *this* is the kind of adult I've grown into. Yes, Portland is less grimy than it used to be but so am I. I wash off my makeup before going to sleep and wake up early to do barre. I wear pants that aren't spandex, rarely order house wine, and say shit like "I need a facial" in complete earnestness.

Unlike my forays into berry picking, I spent the entire truffle journey useless and at the mercy of a dog whose instincts were cultivated in under a year. Doug, the Labrador, found truffle after truffle within patches of, for me, indecipherable dirt. What was a hunt for Doug was a hike for me, and the bounty became a project of meditating on everything the service industry has bestowed to me.

I still and will probably always, in some way, work in a restaurant, which I believe keeps me sharper and my head out of my own ass. Being surrounded by people who are funnier, more talented, and smarter than you every day humbles even the brattiest only child (i.e., me). And though I hope I never stop blowing kisses where Club 21, Magic Gardens, and the Montage once stood, I pray I don't fall victim to my worst sensibilities and close myself off and squander this less beer-soaked milieu of my life or worse yet, side-eyeing the youth who are enjoying this city now, for the first time.

COURSE 1:

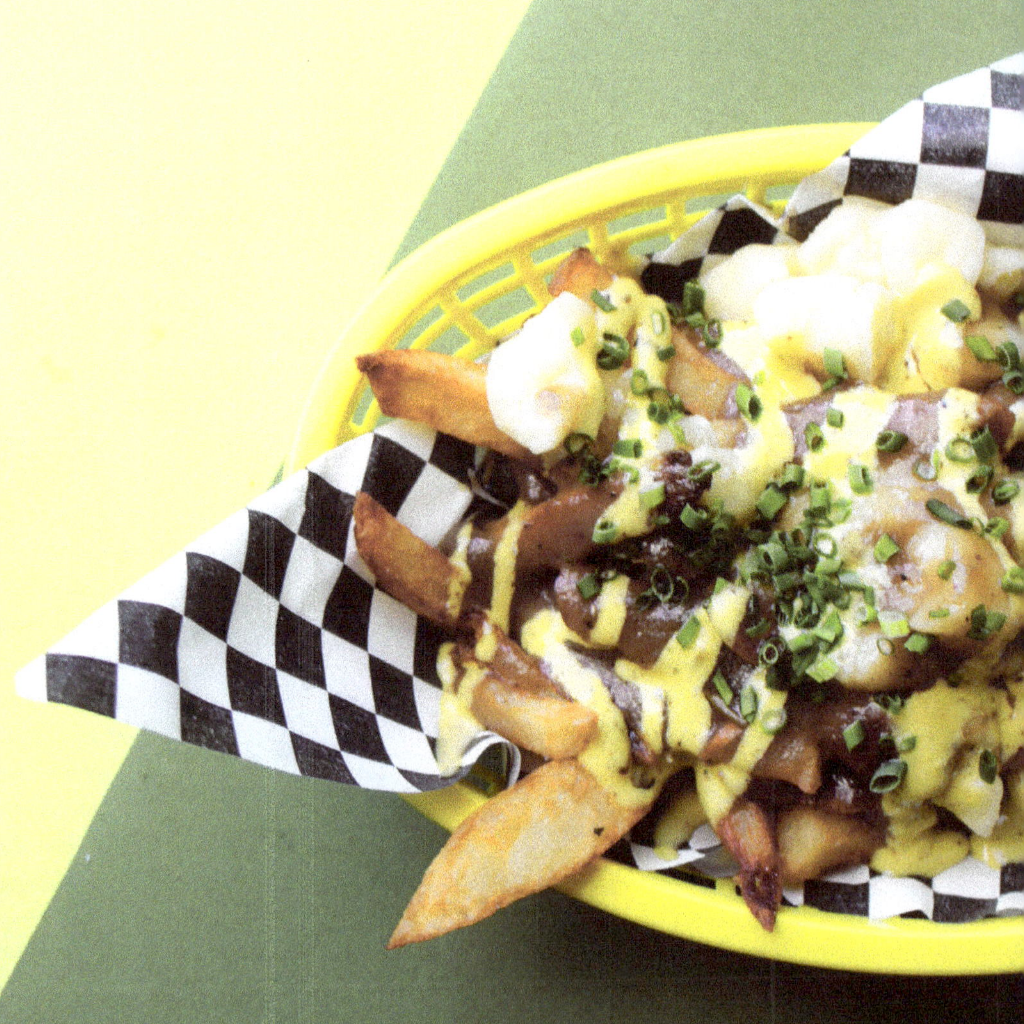

ROSEMARY GRAVY POUTINE WITH TRUFFLE-INFUSED CHEESE CURDS & TRUFFLE AIOLI

An ode to my first job in the service industry, my poutine borrows the profile from the still bumpin' cart on SE 12th and Hawthorne, Potato Champion's *signature sauce (rosemary truffle ketchup). Instead, this recipe infuses the rosemary sprigs into the vinegar-heavy gravy.*

Ingredients

- 6 large russet potatoes, peeled and sliced into ½ thick sticks
- Enough vegetable oil to fill about half of your largest pot, plus more for gravy and roux
- 2 yellow onions, medium chopped
- 2 tablespoons black pepper
- ½ cup balsamic vinegar
- 6 fresh rosemary sprigs
- 4 cups vegetable stock
- ¼ cup rice flour
- 2 cups cheese curds, infused overnight with a truffle nugget
- Chives, diced
- 3 egg yolks
- ½ cup fresh lemon juice
- 3 garlic cloves, grated,
- 1 cup olive oil
- 1 small truffle, shaved
- Salt to taste

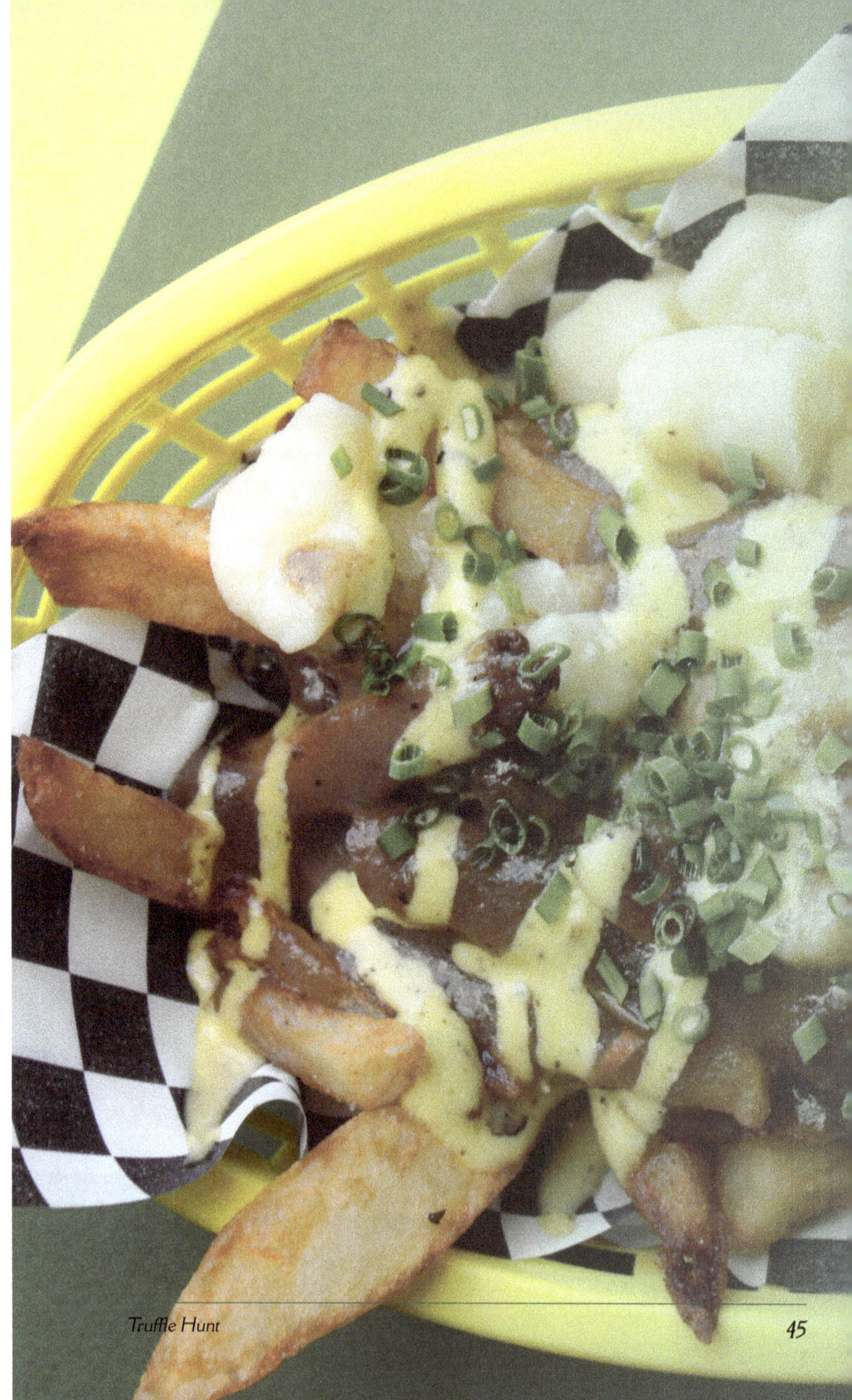

While this is easily the most labor-intensive recipe, most of the prep work can be done well ahead of time. I recommend making the gravy and aioli a day ahead of serving, even allowing the blanched fries to cool up to four hours before their final fry.

In a blender or food processor, blend egg yolks and lemon for thirty seconds, incrementally increasing the speed of your machine. With the blender still on high, drizzle olive oil into the mixture until emulsified. As you slowly reduce the speed, incorporate garlic, truffle shavings and about a teaspoon of salt.

In a large pot, heat 2 tablespoons of vegetable oil over medium heat. Cook onions until they've turned transparent (about four minutes). Season with pepper, then pour balsamic over the onions and continue to sweat them for another three minutes, stirring continually, before drowning them in vegetable stock. Add the rosemary sprigs to infuse. Increase heat to medium-high and simmer until reduced by half.

Meanwhile, in a saucepan, add ¼ cup vegetable oil over medium-high heat, then quickly whisk rice flour into the oil, remove from heat and cool while whisking until the hue turns from a pale white to golden brown.

Reduce the heat under your neighboring pot containing the stock to medium, and pour the rice flour roux in, again whisking quickly. Once the roux is completely incorporated, reduce the heat to medium-low and remove any visible rosemary sprigs. Run an immersion blender throughout the gravy until smooth. Simmer until ready to serve.

Rinse potatoes of their starches by straining them in a colander under cold running water for two minutes, continually jostling them with your hands. Next, pour vegetable oil in your largest pot and, using a cooking thermometer, allow the oil to heat to 350°, working in batches, fry handfuls of potatoes for three minutes before removing from the oil and allowing to sweat on a sheet tray. Repeat until all fries are blanched. In the same pot with the same oil, increase the temperature to 375° and fry potatoes for a second time at the higher temperature for four minutes, again working in small, manageable bunches. Divide your fries into 6 serving bowls, stud the center of each with cheese curds, and ladle a generous amount of gravy over each serving. Garnish with chives, and truffle aioli.

Wine pairing: La Grange Tiphaine Montlouis-Sur-Loire, 2018.

COURSE 2: SOUR CREAM, ONION & TRUFFLE WEDGE SALAD

Though I've never worked at **Clyde's Prime Rib,** ***it's been my pandemic standby, and easily the "old Portland" restaurant I root for and rep most. On my table during every visit to this underrated steakhouse rests an obligatory wedge salad.***

Ingredients

- 1 cup sour cream
- ½ cup buttermilk
- 2 teaspoon onion powder
- 1 medium sized truffle, shaved
- 2 teaspoons salt
- 1 teaspoon black pepper
- 6 quartered iceberg lettuce heads
- 4 slices cooked bacon, finely chopped
- Toasted hazelnuts infused overnight with a small truffle
- 3 eggs, medium boiled, peeled and halved.
- 2 tablespoons chives, diced

In a medium bowl, whisk sour cream and buttermilk with onion powder, shaved truffle, salt and pepper, then allow the truffle to infuse with the fatty dressing for a minimum of 5 hours (can infuse up to three days). Place an iceberg quarter and halved egg on 6 small plates and drizzle your truffle ranch over each wedge. Garnish with bacon bits, hazelnuts, and chives.

Wine pairing: Maloof Wines Beddia Bianco, 2018

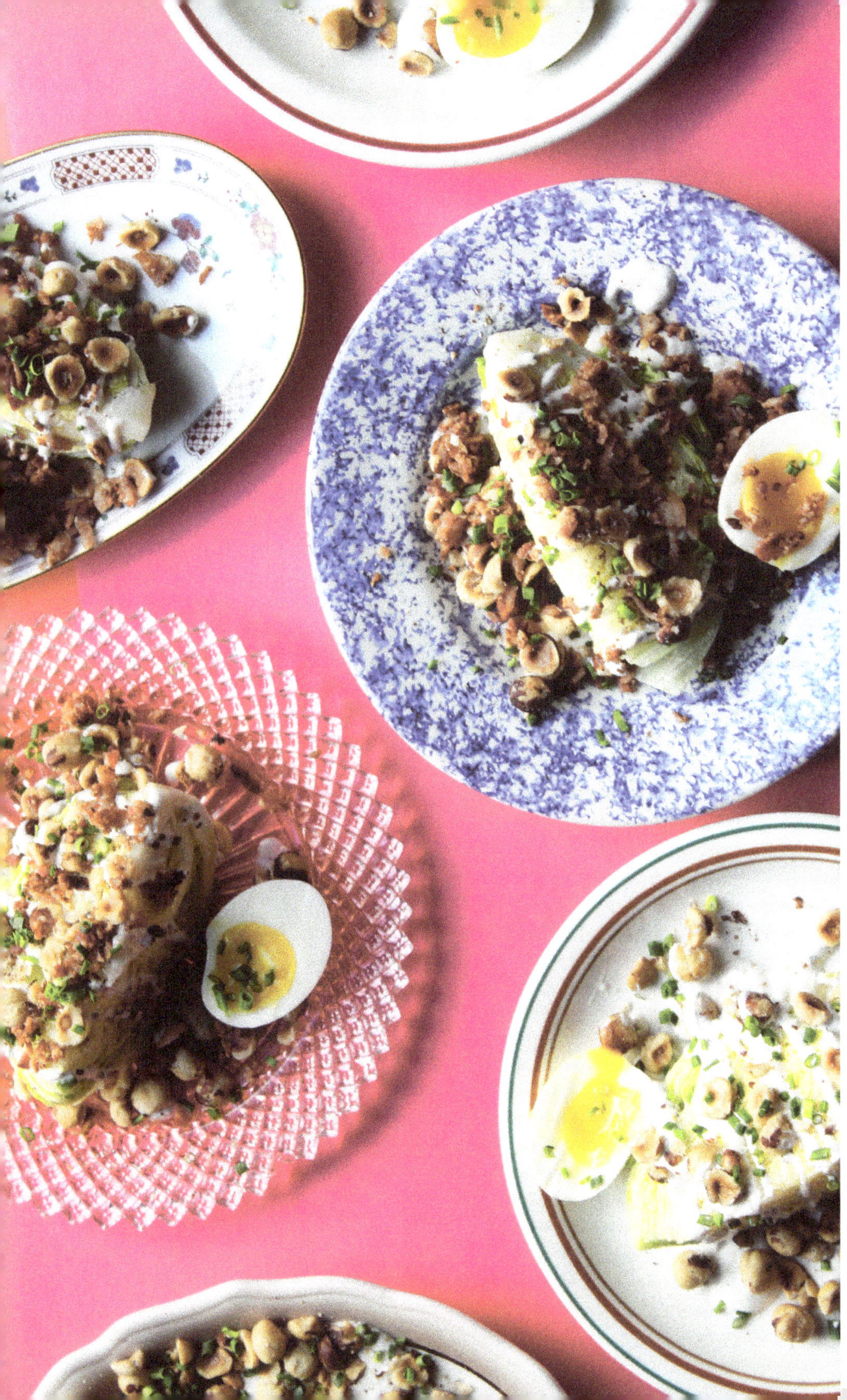

COURSE 3:

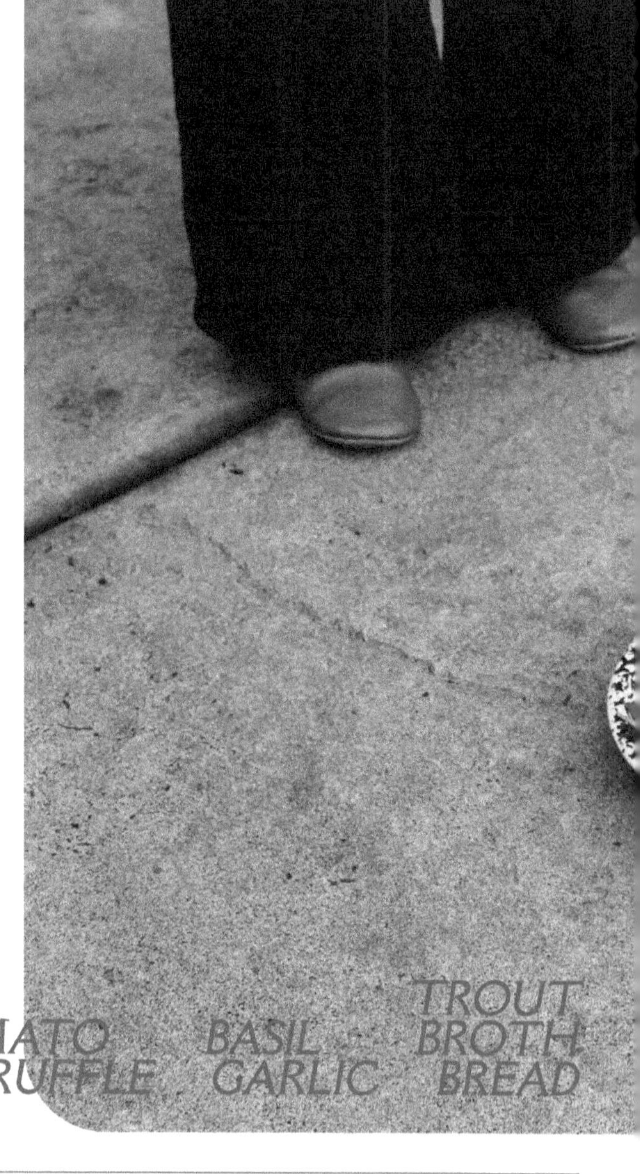

WHOLE TROUT IN TOMATO BASIL BROTH WITH TRUFFLE GARLIC BREAD

The trout in "crazy water" was my first staff meal at The Woodsman Tavern, *and a dish that evokes the early days of my friendship with the woman (Erica Iannitti) who became my best friend and creative collaborator. The garlic bread tips my hat toward the coolest person I met in L.A. (Bryant Gallegos at* Petit Trois*) and the garlic bread we ordered at* The Magic Castle *that never hit the table and still haunts me to this day.*

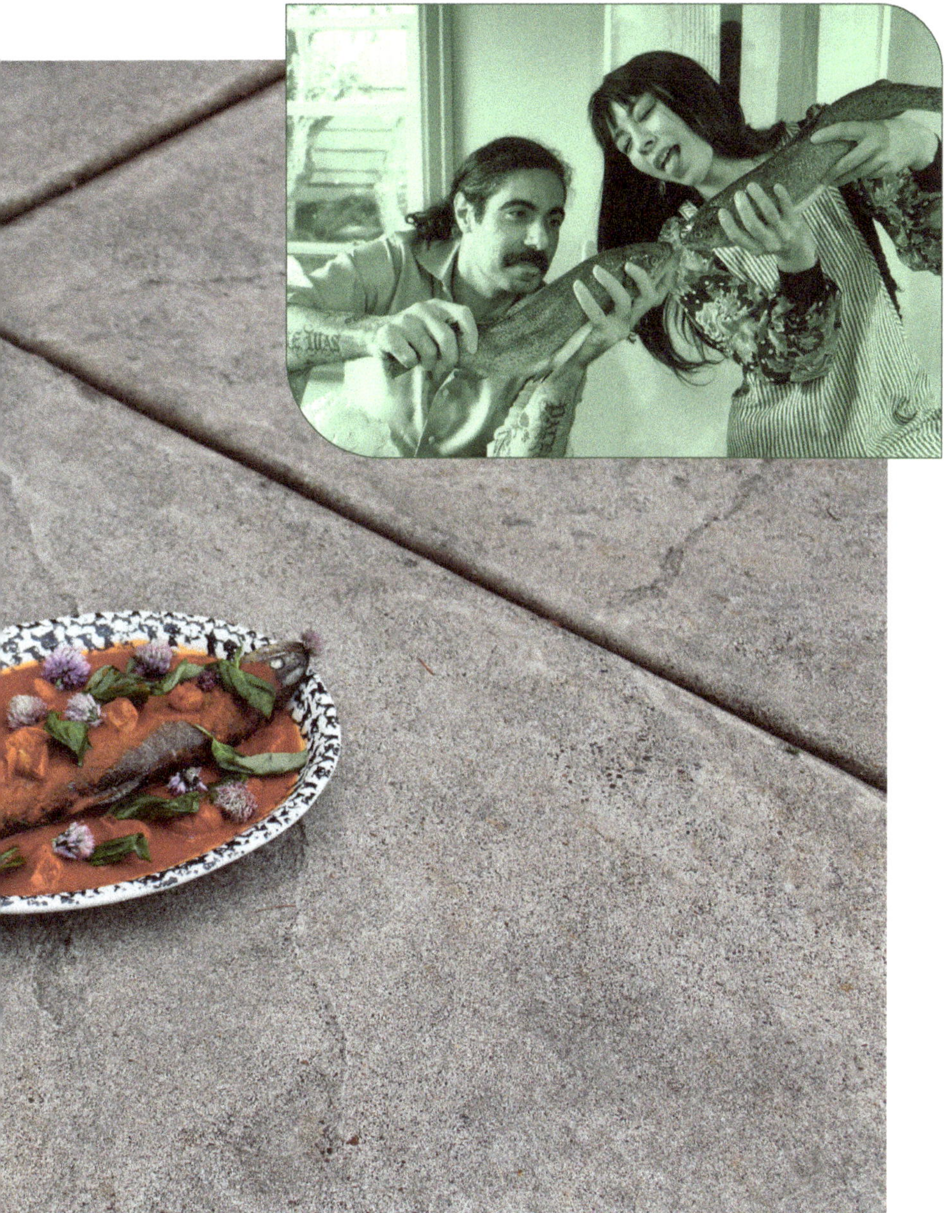

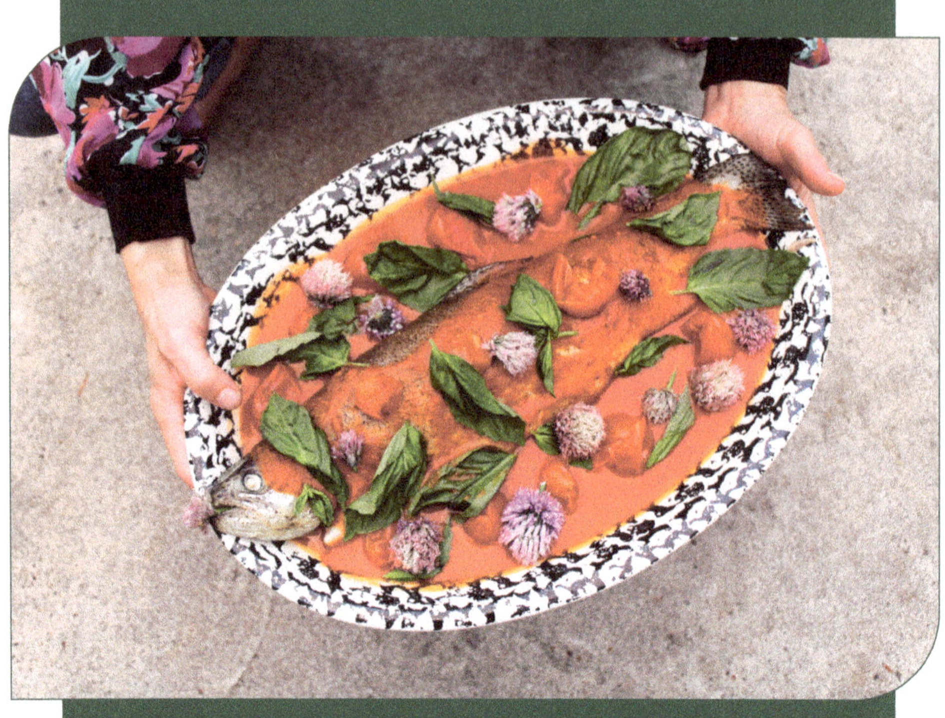

Ingredients

- 1 cup of good olive oil, plus more for broth, cherry tomatoes, and fish
- 1 large shaved truffle
- 1 fennel bulb, finely chopped
- 1 shallot, finely chopped
- 6 garlic cloves, grated
- 1 bunch basil, chopped (plus more to garnish)
- Juice from 1 lemon
- 1 tablespoon tomato paste
- 2 bay leaves
- 2 cups dry (cheap) white wine
- 1 - 28oz can crushed tomatoes
- 2 tablespoons unsalted butter
- 2 - 2lb trout, gutted and cleaned
- 1 pint cherry tomatoes
- 1 bunch purple chive blossoms
- 1 loaf sourdough bread
- 1 tablespoons butter
- ¼ cup fresh parsley, minced
- Kosher salt

To infuse the olive oil, simply sprinkle truffle shavings into the oil and shake. Refrigerate for three days.

For the broth, melt fennel in 2 tablespoons of olive oil over medium-high heat in a large pot. Once limp and aromatic, add shallots, half of the garlic, and 2 teaspoons salt, then cook for another three minutes. As the vegetables absorb the oil, stir in tomato paste, lemon juice, and chopped basil. Increase the temperature to medium-high, then pour white wine into the pot, and cook off the alcohol (about five minutes). Add crushed tomatoes, vegetable broth and bay leaves and reduce to a simmer for at least two hours. Before serving, run an immersion blender through the broth until smooth.

Meanwhile, heat the oven to 375°. Toss cherry tomatoes into a small bowl with 2 teaspoons of salt. Roast tomatoes in a small cast iron skillet for ten to fifteen minutes until they've blistered and burst, set aside.

Slice sourdough loaf in half, vertically, and slather butter and garlic evenly over each side before sprinkling parsley over the butter. Reunite the sides of bread and wrap in tin foil. Bake for ten minutes, remove from the oven, and drizzle with truffle oil just before serving.

Finally, salt each side of both fish while heating 2 tablespoons of olive oil in a large pan. Cook each fish four and a half minutes per side before removing from heat. Allow to rest for an additional five minutes. When ready to serve, place one trout in the center of a large serving dish and spoon tomato broth over the fish until just barely submerged in the liquid. To garnish, dot the plate with blistered tomatoes, torn basil leaves, and chives blossoms. Use your truffle garlic bread to sop up broth.

Wine pairing: Paul-Henri Thilardon Chenas Les Blemonts, 2019

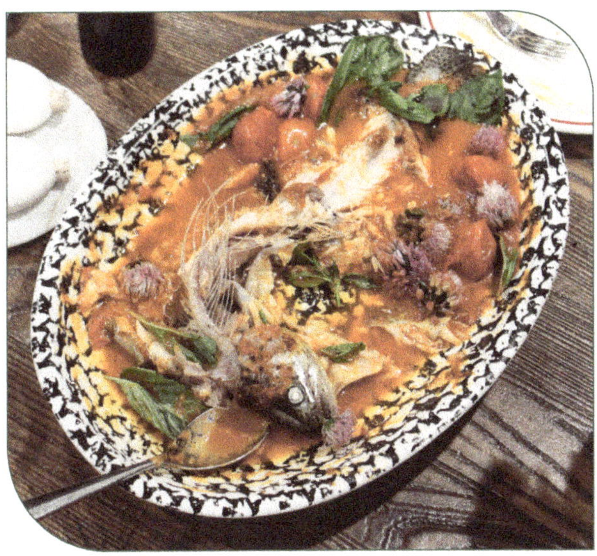

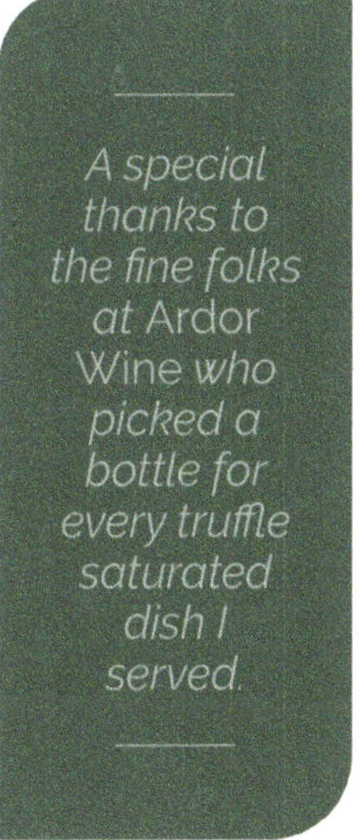

A SEARCHING AND FEAR-LESS MORAL INVENTORY

Words: Jennifer Perrine Art: Dharma Castillo

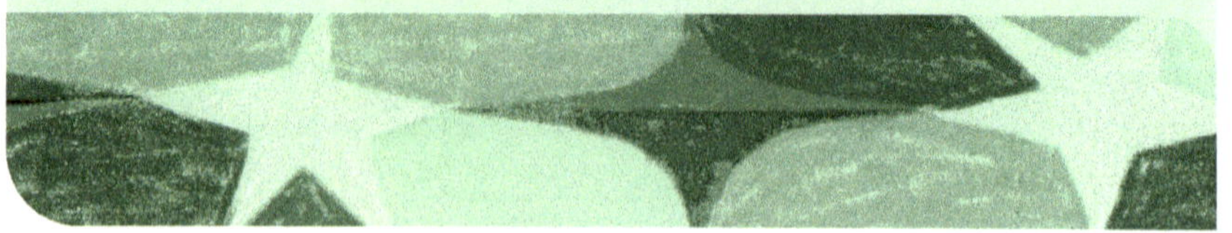

Jennifer Perrine (she/her) is the award-winning author of four books of poetry: *Again, The Body Is No Machine, In the Human Zoo, and No Confession, No Mass.* Their recent short stories and essays appear in *The Gay & Lesbian Review, Valparaiso Fiction Review*, and *Literal Latte*. JP serves as a guest editor for Broadsided Press and a co-editor at Airlie Press, a consensus-based poetry collective. JP lives in Portland, Oregon, where they co-host the Incite: Queer Writers Read series and teach creative writing and intersectional equity practices to youth and adults. To learn more, visit **www.jenniferperrine.org.**

Dharma Castillo (she/her) was born in Miami, Florida of immigrant parents. Her parents drove her across country in a shoebox as an infant where they settled in Beaverton, Oregon. Her young mother with no sitter often brought her along to Portland State design classes. She believes her love of color and figurative arts stems from both her Latin roots and the dynamic culture of Portland.

Instagram: @**another.portland.artist**

I was ashamed to be seen with my mother in public, not in the way that all daughters are—embarrassed by the smothering touch, the nonchalance with which she discusses personal items, the way she announces in front of any crowd that you need a new bra or more tampons or a fresh tube of acne cream. I would have begged heaven for a mother like that. No, I was ashamed because my mother was a drunk—not the functional kind who went to work and returned and no one was the wiser that she'd been nipping at gin all day, or even the sort who stayed home with the babies and finished a bottle of white wine before any diapers got changed. My mother was the type of drunk who had lost her license, and so I had to drive her to work. At fifteen, I had a learner's permit and was technically fine to make the drive out, my mother rifling through her purse in the passenger seat, but then I had to risk the trip home unaccompanied and hope I wouldn't get pulled over.

At her job, no one cared that my mother was a drunk. She served beers at the lone bar in town, the one that sold tight t-shirts and thongs with *I got lucky at the Lucky Seven* emblazoned across the chest or crotch in cheap iron-on decals that would crack and start to rub off after the first wash. I knew this because my mother brought the bar's merch home for me instead of buying me real clothes. I wore my jean jacket buttoned up every day at school, but still everyone knew that underneath I was wearing some variant of the Lucky Seven logo.

My mother drank most of her tips, something that her boss encouraged, and she'd been known to call me at closing to let me know she didn't need a ride home, that she'd be staying with Jerry or Roger or Butch tonight. I didn't care too much that she slept with so many men—my dad was dead, and she was lonely, so why not?—but some of those men were my classmates' fathers, the ones who'd left their mothers, who never ponied up for child support, spending their meager wages on another round or on the jukebox. *Deadbeats*, my best friend Max called them, and she ought to have known. Her father was one of the Rogers.

***

My mom was ashamed to be seen with me, all those years later, after she'd been collecting chips at AA meetings, after rock bottom, which she said she hit on the night Roger convinced her to go swimming in the river in February, in Vermont. The ice had thawed, and the two besotted lovebirds were convinced it would be fine, warm enough in the sunlight. My mom was swept downriver, concussed by a rock, found naked by a nurse walking home from work who just happened to spot her crumpled on the shore. Roger had run off. The nurse said my mom was so blue she assumed she was dead. When she woke up, detoxing in the hospital, she said she knew it was time to get clean. To her credit, she stuck to it, all those years of sobriety, of making amends.

My mom's years of drinking were wiped clean by grace, by the glittery sobriety coins that marked her abstinence. She carried them in her purse, and I could hear them clatter when she sat down in the chair farthest from the sofa that Max and I shared. We had sent the wedding announcements only last week, and Max and I had our worst fight yet over whether to invite my mom. "Would you invite Roger?" I'd asked.

Max didn't yell. She never yelled, but I knew she wanted to. "I don't have a dad, remember? He walked out and never tried to come back. Your mom sobered up. She called you all the time after the accident, asking for forgiveness." *The accident*, that's what Max always called my mom's choice to skinny-dip in winter. "Give her a break," Max said, and when that didn't work, she mailed off the invitation against my wishes.

When my mom called, she said she had to meet us at our house, not at a diner or café, as Max had suggested, knowing it would decrease the chance of a scene. "First time for everything," I said when my mother drove two towns over to visit us. We'd lived there six years. I'd been surprised when she pulled into our drive—I had been a child the last time I'd seen her behind the wheel, before those years I drove her around, before she kicked me out when she caught me in bed with Max.

"You would have left anyway," Max always said when I brought up that, in all her attempts to make amends, my mom had never once apologized for taking my key and banishing me. I had to break a window and sneak in to get my clothes and schoolbooks and the uniform I wore to work. My mom had called the cops, tried to have me arrested for breaking and entering. I'd lucked out—one of the cops was dating Max's mom and knew the whole situation. Max's mom, Irene, had let me sleep on her couch after I got kicked out, and later, even in Max's bed, after she'd had time to wrap her head around Max being gay. Irene had always been sweet to me, and even bought me new shirts when I started wearing Max's clothes. "Just so the town doesn't talk too much," she said, meaning she was doing her best to keep us safe. She knew how quickly gossip traveled in this town and what doors it closed, and if it weren't for her, who knew whose side the police would have taken.

My mom didn't talk to me again until sometime after her white chip, when she started making the calls to apologize. Even then, she insisted that what Max and I had together was a sin, that she knew this even more clearly now that she was sober and could tell right from wrong. "I'll pray for you," she said, and I got tired of hearing it.

And then she was in our living room. She'd aged poorly, ruddy-faced, eyelids of melted wax. Still, she looked like my mom. She lit a cigarette even after I asked her not to. "Do you have to go through with this? It was bad enough when you moved in together. I could tell people you were roommates, but now..." She shifted, plucking at her pale peach dress, something she must have worn that morning to church. Max and I, heathens in our jeans and t-shirts, tried to explain.

"We're not looking for your blessing," I said.

Max put a hand on my leg, cut me off. "It would mean so much to us if you would come," she said. "We've been together for eight years, and we just want our families to be there when we make it official."

My mom pulled the invitation from her purse, read it over, tapped it against her knee. "Why do you have to have it in Haven Park?" she said. "Where anyone could see? Can't you just keep this"—she waved her hand around, sweeping up the space Max and I shared—"Can't you keep it private?"

I must have screamed when I slapped her, when I upended her purse to find those clattering chips, spilled them on the floor and stomped on them. My

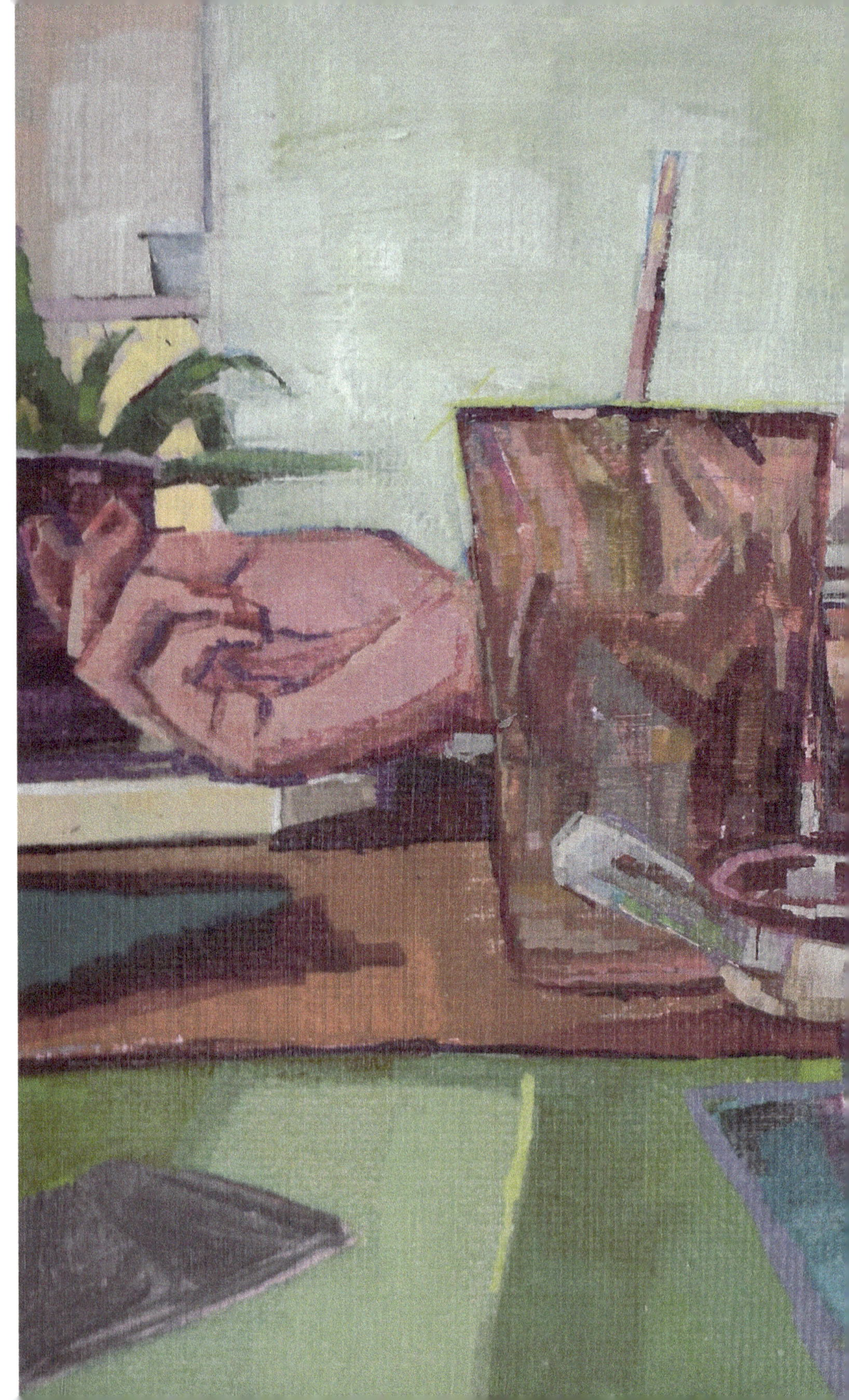

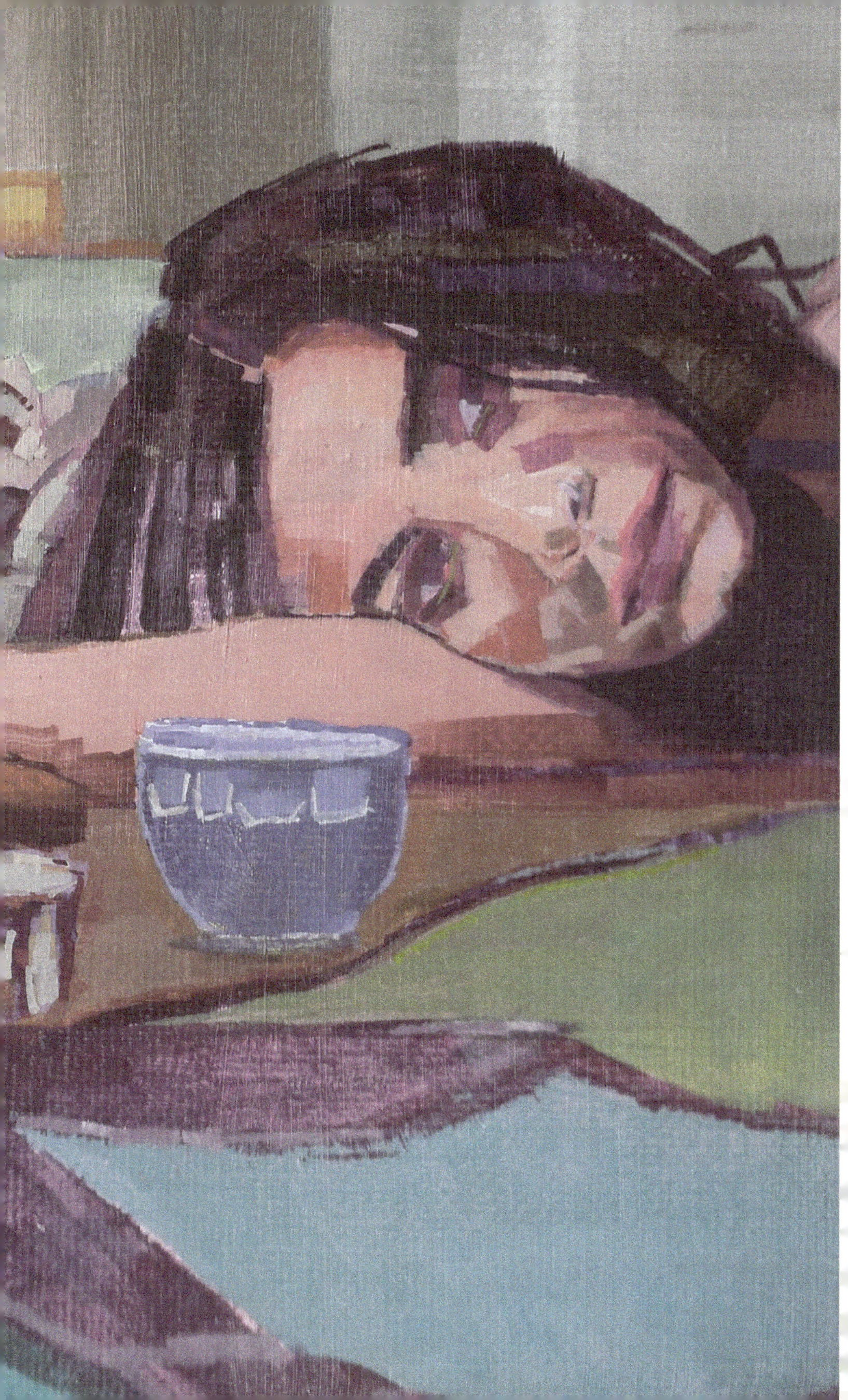

throat hurt for weeks after. I was so hoarse Max said she could barely hear me when I made my vows.

***

Neither Mom nor I wanted to be seen with each other. Mom told me I looked like a man. "You're not the girl I gave birth to" is how she said it, as I pushed her chair through the mall.

I wished I'd left her in the nursing home as I had for the last few years, after she'd become too frail to manage on her own. But her chaplain had been calling me to let me know how my mother's mind had been slipping further and faster lately, a leaky sieve. "Soon, she may not remember you at all," the chaplain said the last time we talked.

"Do you know why I don't visit?" I'd asked.

"Your mother may have a problem with it, but I don't," the chaplain said, matter of fact. "She might not even remember you're gay at this point."

It was hard to tell if she did or not, though she certainly didn't like the looks of me.

"Too much swagger," she said, "like the men who thought they could pick me up just by looking at me, back in my bar days."

They could, I thought. *They did*, but I didn't say so. Time hadn't been kind to Mom. It was hard to believe she was the same age as Irene, who'd married that cop, who still sent Christmas cards and birthday gifts even now that Max and I had divorced. I still ran into Irene jogging around Haven Park or having brunch with her friends or shopping, as Mom and I were doing now, at the newly built mall.

I'd wanted to stay at the nursing home, where the staff could deflect tension, could give Mom something to focus on other than me, but Mom insisted. "I want to go for a drive," she said. "I miss driving." I had folded her chair into my trunk and let one of the aides ease Mom into the front seat. We drove slowly, aimlessly, through the snow, both of us silent, the radio chopping songs as the reception cut in and out. The mall was my idea, a way to fill the void, the long wall of nothing that stretched between us. I couldn't stand Mom when I was young and she was a drunk, but at least I knew who she was. Now, she was just an old woman I rolled through the mall, tinny Christmas music tinkling around us although it wasn't even December yet.

"Stop here," Mom said, pointing at the store that sold dollar jewelry, baubles aimed at teen girls. The chair wouldn't fit down the slim aisles, so I pushed it up to one of the front racks filled with dangly earrings and faux silver charms. Mom had worn jewelry like this when I was a kid, but now she went unadorned, a baggy dress slumped over her, her thinned hair pulled back in a taut, stringy bun.

She pulled a pair of bronze hoops off the rack, careful to cup them in her bloated fingers. She held them up to me. "Do you think my daughter would like these?" she asked.

I would never have gone in for such ugly things. "Yes, I'm sure she would," I said.

Mom frowned at me, put the hoops down in her lap.

"Do you want to buy those?" I asked, unsure if I should help her slide them back on the rack.

"You know," she said, "it's a shame you and Max couldn't work things out."

I wasn't sure I'd heard her right. "We tried," I said at last. "I had a temper." *Understatement*, I thought. "I went to the anger management classes like she asked me to, but by then it was too late." Why was I telling her this? Did she really wish Max and I were together? *Maybe I should call Max*, I thought, *ask her to meet me for coffee, nothing special.* I owed her an apology, or a dozen apologies, and maybe I could work up the courage to say so.

"Max was such a lovely young girl, Roger. You could have been a better father to her," Mom said, fumbling with the earrings until they dropped to the floor. "She needed a man like you in her life. If she'd had you around, she might not have turned out—"

It took all the strength I had to walk away from her then, to call the chaplain to come get her, not to hit this old woman with the tired face that held in it some memory of my mother.

a l t . a n g s t

Words: Hope Del Carlo Art: Myra Lilith Day

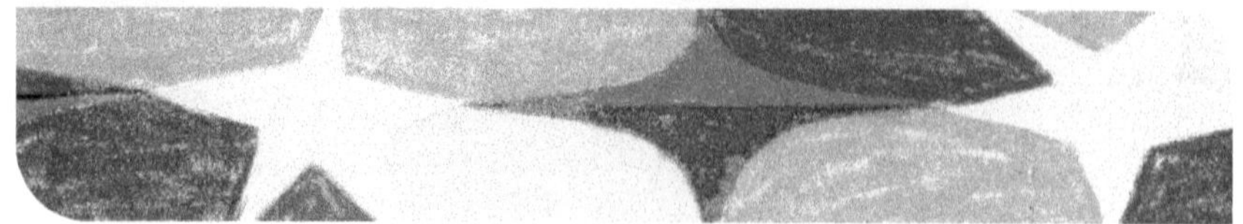

Hope Del Carlo (she/her) is a consumer protection lawyer and rabbit owner. She lives in Portland with her current husband, Joe Johnson, and a rotating cast of their five kids.

Incompleteness is often regarded as failure, but Myra Lilith Day (she/her) positions it as an ever-expanding potential for change. Her work is an act of refusal, rejecting the prescribed use of the technologies she engages. Day accretes digital techniques around her experience of gender non-conforming womanhood, combining coding, 3D modeling, and game design in ways which defy traditional measures of success. Being visibly queer can be burdensome and exhausting, as we live in an era when social media and surveillance culture are constantly evolving to more intimately capture the details of our private selves. Day engages digital practice to ameliorate the feeling of exposure caused by the increased visibility of queerness in a world still unsafe for queer people.

Website: **myralilithday.com**
Instagram: **@myralilithday**
Itch.io: **myralilithday**

Email was the first thing I knew about the internet. I couldn't fathom why anyone used email when it meant sitting in front of a gigantic machine, locked in a computer lab. Electronic mail was textureless compared to the sepia-toned letters I wrote to my friends in Santa Fe, Seattle, and Santa Cruz with my frippy fountain pen. My boyfriend, Jim, was in engineering school at Cal Poly in San Luis Obispo at the time. He and his friends used email and they were huge dorks.

Later, stranded at home in rural California after college, I started using email regularly and really learned how to embarrass myself online. My hometown barely had cable TV, but around 1994 I talked my mom into dial-up internet service through a local ISP that one of my techy friends had set up with his dad.

This was a drifting time for me. I was lonely. As soon as we had internet access, I discovered Usenet groups. If you missed the internet's gooey phase, circa 1994-1997, Usenet groups were a series of topical, threaded chat rooms; a primordial social medium with no pictures or memes, just user-generated text.

I liked to lurk in a Usenet group called alt.angst. The posters there were miserable—angsty—and they used pseudonyms, so they could complain about bosses, exes, and bad friends without any social consequences. They compared their anti-depressant prescriptions and shrinks. They talked each other out of committing suicide, collectively wringing their hands over whether to call 911 on certain posters. I think some of them may have met each other in real life (or, "IRL," as they called it). IRL seemed like the wrong direction to me. Keeping it all on alt.angst was better, I thought, because it could be by turns private and public, secretive and exhibitionistic; a glory hole for tortured souls. It felt like I had found a secret goth literary circle, a substitute for my handful of melancholy friends who were doing more useful things with their early twenties. It was the closest thing to Dorothy Parker's Algonquin Round Table I could find.

I was addicted to it, spending hours wallowing in strangers' horrible lives, drafting my own confessions and then not posting them. The standards for publicizing angsty-ness were extremely high, as evidenced by the group's FAQs, which warned that, *"alt.angst does not tolerate cheeriness in any form. . . If you feel inclined to post any stories with a happy ending, post them to alt.good.news, or some other forum — perhaps alt.romance.chat. You'll be lucky if other members use such kind words to tell you to do the same."* I took these warnings seriously and stayed mostly quiet, afraid of showing my intermittently optimistic underbelly.

I learned to love the internet's apparent anonymity. I thought I was invisible there. Finally, I was free to be my worst self, but in an artsy way. I was still afraid, but it wasn't the usual fear--that my sadness and anxiety wouldn't be accepted. That was something alt.angst actually wanted from me. My fear was more like performance anxiety that my presentation skills weren't up to snuff. But performance was something I could work on. My essentially discontented nature hadn't found a home in "meatspace," as the cynical techies were starting to call the living world. The risk-free world of the internet, however, might think I was okay, as depressed and anxious and skin-picking as I was.

I thought, then, that the internet was going to be a place to see, be seen, and at the same time, to hide, to watch, and be watched without *really* being watched. It was an endlessly liminal space, I thought—a place where you could express important things without risking any important consequences. A place to try on the truth, even the ugly truth, like a diary that you could show people without them remembering it. Sort of like having access to the zapper in *Men in Black* that makes people forget they've seen aliens.

I finally did post a few bits on alt.angst; I don't remember what they were about; probably my issues with God and my parents and rural life. I got some feedback from the other lost people on there. Nobody flamed me. I saved my posts for a while. They made me feel like a writer.

Emboldened, I started exploring the web a little more. Jim's friends at Cal Poly were learning HTML and starting websites of their own, since they seemed to know where the world was headed.

Jim had this roommate, Tim, who I had met a few times during school vacations, when I'd visited Jim in SLO. Tim is now a good adult; an engineer, happy husband, and father of two. But twenty-two-year-old Tim was bemused by his libido and his maleness. Famous even among computer lab-dwelling nerds for his thriftiness, he would cook an entire box of spaghetti and store it in a giant Tupperware container, then eat it glopped with cold Ragu for a week. He elevated the pragmatic over the aesthetic.

Tim and Jim shared a bedroom in their dorm apartment, and when I visited, Jim kicked Tim out of their shared room. He had to sleep on the living room couch. I think this made him angry.

When the internet was born a few years later, Tim put up an early website, and Jim told me about it. This was dial-up time, so nothing loaded quickly. I would go to Tim's page and sit in stupefied ecstasy while it loaded, left to right, line by line, incrementally filling the screen.

Tim's page had color, the bluish, greenish shade computer geeks called cyan, as I had learned in a BASIC class during sixth grade summer school. It loaded so slowly. So, so slowly, text would appear, and then a photo, bit by bit by bit, block by block.

Tim's website was not startling or controversial. The image that loaded on Tim's page, after many minutes of waiting, was a heartwarmingly boring photo of Tim with his English bulldog.

Looking at this image on the emerging World Wide Web, still attached to its virtual placenta, I was thunderstruck.

If Tim had mailed me a print of himself with his dog, well, I would have thought he was really slipping. I would have looked at it once and stuffed it into a drawer with the floppy disks. But on the internet, with that revelatory cyan background, and the portent of the future swirling in my imagination, the photo of Tim and his dog was, literally, a window into the New World.

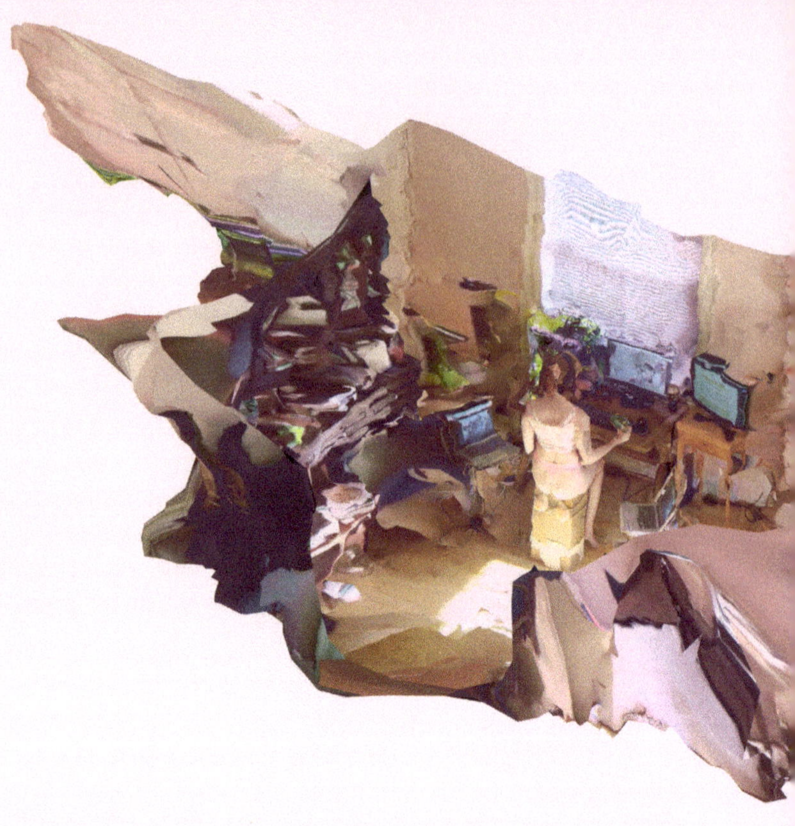

The *New* New World.

I couldn't get enough. I looked at Tim's website for several days in a row. I'd go to his page, sit in rapt silence for twelve or thirteen minutes while it slowly came into being, and marvel, like it was a time-lapse of the birth of the universe.

On some level, I knew I was doing something weird. But I was under the terrible misapprehension that I was looking into a consequence-free world. I thought a web page was like alt.angst, a place where I could raise or lower the scrim of anonymity to suit my risk-tolerance. I thought if I didn't tell Tim, and if he wasn't in the room with me, that he wouldn't know I was staring at him. And his dog.

This was a short-lived delusion.

After many days in a row of worshipping at Tim's website, I was surprised to check my email and see a message from him in there. It was odd enough that I didn't even think to worry before I opened it.

"Wow," Tim's message said. "Thirty-seven page views in four days." I sucked my breath in. My eyelids widened.

"Is it me or the dog that keeps you coming back?"

There are moments of mortification that never leave you, not for your

Angel on Computer *(from the web art installation* **"An Angel in 3/4 View"***). Scan QR code to experience the installation in full.*

whole life. The cold blood pools in your hands. The face sweats. Digestion stops.

I died. I died death. I fell over and I died. Then I got up and read the email again. And died again. And again.

I had been seen by Tim. And his dog, oh, the dog. They saw me staring, watching them, stupid in my unselfconscious wonderment. I had harshly judged Tim's nerdiness and pasta-eating habits, and now the shoe was on the other foot. Tim had unequivocal proof that I was much, much weirder than he was, in every way imaginable. I was the world's strangest, creepiest dog and dork stalker. I hit my personal angst bottom.

I didn't realize before that moment that, unlike the paper page, the page on the internet has eyes behind it. I didn't know what an IP address was. I didn't know about hit counters. Still, the scales had fallen from my eyes. I knew, then, that the internet is not a placeless place of anonymity. Someone in there sees you looking. The anonymity is fake, a one-way mirror. You gaze into the abyss and it really does gaze back, to paraphrase Nietzsche, or some other old philosopher who never embarrassed himself on the internet. From inside the abyss, the watcher laughs.

My safe place to put my secrets was gone. Now I knew that it wasn't safe. It's public, and worse, it's permanent. Whatever it captures never goes away. I have been on listservs where people take oaths to keep posts confidential. Because of Tim and his dog, I don't trust that. Anything emailed or posted on a listserv is as public as broadcast radio, and way more likely to be saved in service of evil.

You would think that after my humiliation in the '90s, I would always remember that the internet is watching, but over long years of acclimation, I am sometimes still nonchalant about it. The delusion that we have privacy online is persistent. I tell myself that there is no privacy there, but I forget over and over again.

In early 2013, soon after Sandy Hook, beside myself with frustration at our inability to do anything about mass shootings, I posted on the Moms Demand Action Facebook group about Target's unwillingness to ask people to leave their stores when they came in openly carrying guns. It wasn't a threatening post or anything like that—I just bragged that I had moved all of my prescriptions away from Target, and I wasn't setting foot in their stores again until they changed their policy that allowed people to carry huge guns around while they shopped.

Then something weird happened. For several years after I made that post, whenever I would Google myself, that post, along with my name and Facebook profile picture, would appear in the search results. Nothing else I had ever posted on Facebook showed up—just that.

I realized, after a few years, that the repost wasn't random. Someone had intentionally made my Facebook message visible to the world at large, so that anyone who was interested in me as a potential friend, as a date, as a candidate for a job, would know where I stood on the open carrying of firearms in Target. Someone was trying to hurt me by publicizing my opinion more broadly than I had cast it. Someone I didn't even know. The anonymity I had enjoyed was turned back on me by someone who loved the Second Amendment. It scared me.

I still use the internet. I sit in front of my Mac, with its built-in webcam, doing whatever. I trust that if the little green light isn't on, it isn't live-streaming me straight to a pay-by-the minute cam site (nosepickmilf.com), but it could be. Other times, I'm paranoid and believe that my phone, the internet's bratty little lackey, is listening to everything I do and say, then generating targeted ads that spookily correspond with my thoughts. I ask my friend if his wife is at the Sou'wester Lodge, and a few hours later, my Facebook feed contains a Willamette Week article about the Sou'wester Lodge from four years ago. Could that be a coincidence?

I put my phone on my nightstand and wonder what else it's tracking. Would it even help to turn it off? Somebody probably knows; none of my tech-savvy friends, even the ones who work for Big Evil Tech, are giving up their smartphones.

This is the easily researched part of what is now scary about the internet. I've avoided learning too much about data mining, personalized search results, and the other parade of Brave New World horribles my kids tell me about. I don't want to know enough to worry about any of that.

A year's worth of my online bank statements is no more me than a year's worth of flushed toilet paper. There is a part of me that the internet can't touch, and I know it. I guess I'd call it my soul. My working hypothesis is that the soul is everything about you that can't be found on the internet. The body. Private thoughts. If I were to fully believe that the internet can steal my essence, I would be lost. Turn the internet off and I can feel my blank personhood accumulating again, like quiet goose down being blown into a comforter. Instead of identifying that feeling as boredom or anxiety, I think those feelings of stuffy emptiness have value. That shaky unknown is worth my attention. Something wells up when I have no contact, no input. It's a connection with myself.

The internal voice can grow unfamiliar, so that when I hear it after long absence, it scares me. It sounds like a ghost, the Holy Spirit, the ancestors. Whatever I call it, it is there. But the sensation of making contact with it has changed for me. It is more difficult now--more difficult to get there, and harder to enjoy it. I have felt weirdly enervated since 2007, when I got my first iPhone. I don't think it's just because I'm part of the jaded and numb Generation X. Whatever touch or love or acceptance I thought I was getting from the internet in my alt.angst days has been undone by the toll the internet has taken on my ability to just sit around in the world. Quitting smoking seventeen years ago was easier than quitting the absent-minded flick through my Facebook feed. It has become an escape from which I cannot escape. A phony solitude in which I am never really alone. A community to which I am never really connected. It is the death mask of life—a cold, un-breathing, un-hearing yet always-listening thief of our attention.

We have had the printed page for centuries. Does it also separate us from life? Last year, my husband Joe and I went to a lecture by an expert in Yiddish newspapers. The speaker put up a slide of a room full of teenaged girls in the 1920s, each of them looking at their own copy of the same newspaper, wanting to be photographed that way, not acknowledging the camera or each other, just reading. It reminded me of these days, the everyday sight of a roomful of kids looking at their phones. I instantly feel judgy about this kind of scene. What is it I think they're supposed to be paying attention to? What are we all supposed to be looking at?

I guess we're supposed to be looking at everything. Even the tedious and painful things. All witnessing, without a filter, has inherent holy value. Observation is something only living things can do; the way we look at things is the essence of reality. There's always temptation to reach outside of life for its interpretive gloss, rather than just living; it's all dead if it can't take us back into the flow and force of life. This is where we find soul.

LOST ONES

Words: Willow Fields Art: Tara Murino-Brault

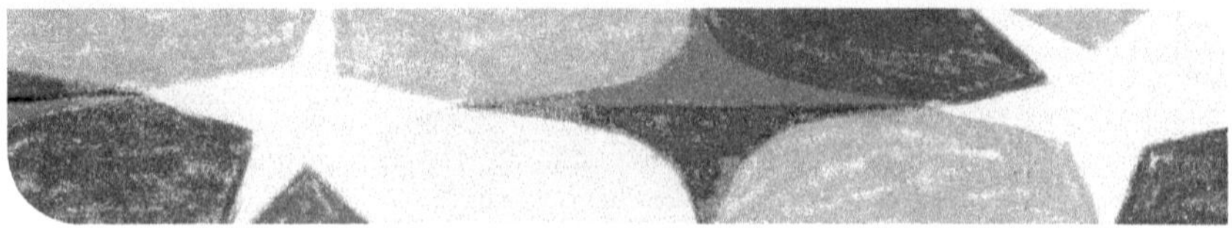

Willow Fields (he/him), comfortable in his adopted home of Washington State, maintains a humble writing and recording practice from his cramped, sound-treated closet. With sponge-like attentiveness, he continually strives to incorporate distant subject matters, from grotesque literature, to Virtual Reality, to everyday, mundane errands into his lifelong passion for fiction. An emerging writer with a vibrant inclination towards the satirical, ridiculous and darkly-otherworldly, he has had work previously appear in the *In Parenthesis Magazine* and *The Dillydoun Review*. His stories (including self-produced, flash fiction narrations) can be found on Facebook or Instagram under **Willow's Field** or **Willows_Field**, respectively.

Tara Murino-Brault (she/they) was born and raised in Chicago. She received her BFA in Graphic Design at The University of Illinois at Chicago and her MFA in printmaking and book arts at the Minneapolis College of Art and Design. Currently, she is an artist and educator who resides in the Portland Oregon area with her wife, Emily and their fourteen-year-old son named Gus. She teaches a variety of classes at Portland Community College. As a maker, her favorite mediums are all forms of printmaking, book arts, laser cutting, and wood sculpture.

Website: **taramurinobrault.com**
Instagram: **@thesneakyfox1**

My friend was lost in the woods. I don't know how she happened to be lost, exactly. We were there a year before during a field trip with our college course, 'History of the Northwest.' We had both roamed the many trails, even found our way to the beach—at the time, accompanied by our other classmates and a chaperoning, herbal-scented professor. But now, there was no one else with me. No one else to help search for my friend, who was lost in the woods.

It seemed like only a few minutes since I had begun my search. Only a few minutes since I deposited my bike at the trailhead, where I had the gut-wrenching realization that my Gary Fisher was the only one there. I knew for certain that my friend had ridden a bike that gloomy, overcast day. Fleetingly, I also failed to see any cars in the gravel parking lot. My lone mountain bike was the closest thing to a vehicle at the trailhead. Scouring the woods for my friend I assumed I was the closest thing to a conscious being in the sprawling thicket of pines and cedars.

It felt like only a few minutes since I began my search, but at a glance, my watch told me more than an hour had passed since I stepped into the woods. My worry spurred by the sudden, almost irrational jump in time, I quickened my pace. My footfalls slammed against the earth in time to my pounding heart.

Although there was only one main trail head, there were many trails through the woods; far too many possible avenues my friend could have lost herself down. Luckily, the woods weren't particularly thick, the trees well-spaced out and the ground brush sparse. The plot of land, however, was slopped and hilly. At many moments, I couldn't see the other trails from the one on which I was walking. I wanted to be thorough, to increase my chances, so I hurriedly walked them all.

I hadn't been calling my friend's name, at first, because I had a dreadful, numbing notion that if I did, the woods would more deliberately hide her from me. My anxiety told me to stay quiet, to avoid disrupting the natural stillness that the vegetation projected around me. That the woods were sentient, conscious, sounds ridiculous—I know—but in the moment, it felt all too true.

Eventually, I convinced myself to break my vow of silence, cast off my muffling shroud of dread and loudly called her name. "HOLLY!"

The woods came alive. A great whisper went through the trees, as if a gale force wind were rippling their branches, swaying their trunks. I felt no wind. Birds chirped and fluttered their wings in the intangible breeze, insects buzzed, and the old moss-bearded trees groaned ominously. The air smelled of damp and dirt, crisp pine and salty, ocean tides. The underbrush rustled with the movement of unseen critters.

I yelled out my friend's name again and the woods fell abruptly silent once more. It was as if I had flipped a light switch quickly on, then off. But there was still one disturbance. Twigs snapped and leaves rustled as something large rushed through the bushes, down the hill and towards me. From my angle, I could not see who or what it was. My hopeful mind jumped quickly to Holly—maybe she heard me, maybe she was not as lost as I feared; my anxious heart conjured images of massive predators, bears and wolves and cougars, hurtling through the foliage. As the rustling grew closer, however, I

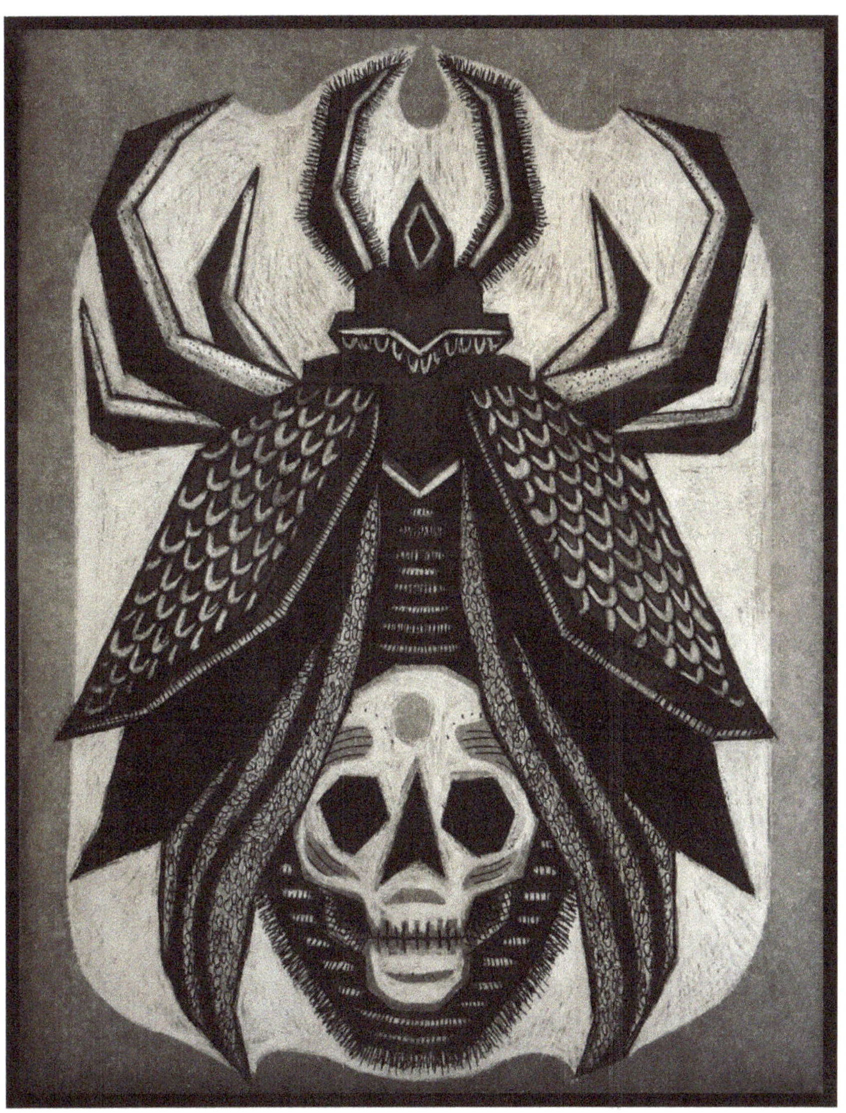

Skull Bug.

quickly saw it was neither my friend nor a carnivorous beast.

It was a man. He looked to be in his late forties, with thinning hair and a panicked, sad look plastered on his face. "Please," he said as he stumbled onto the trail in front of me, "I have lost my son. Can you help?"

Calming my racing heart, I explained to him that I had also lost my friend. I told him that I had been searching for her for more than an hour.

The man, panting, catching his breath, gave me a most pitiful look. He shook his head woefully and said, "I think my son has been lost for over day."

Incredulous, I looked him up and down in that moment and asked what I thought to be the most obvious question. "How?" After a brief pause, I added, "You have no food or water and you've been searching for over a day?"

He looked back at me with a deep-seated terror in his eyes. "I do not know," he said, "I do not understand it—I-I am diabetic and have not had to take insulin this entire time. I have not been hungry or thirsty..." He trailed off and looked at his own watch before concluding confusedly, "It has felt like only few hours..."

The unease I had been tolerating since realizing my friend was possibly lost doubled, tripled, and took a deeper hold with an ironclad grip. Shrugging off their differences, my heart and mind formed a united front of anxiety, forcing a worried bead of sweat to trickle down my brow. The man's words nagged at me. They attempted to remind me of a foggy responsibility I couldn't quite recall in the moment. I was forgetting something, but the surging waves of worry that swept over me washed away my struggles to remember; I could only focus on one idea, one question: Where is my friend?

The man and I decided to join forces. We walked the trails together, alternating between who chose which path to go down and which ones we double-backed on when new trails didn't appear. We also began alternatingly calling out the names of our lost ones and, for the first few rounds, nothing happened. But as I called my friend's name for the sixth time, the woods became alive again. The leaves whispered and rustled and the old trees groaned once more, but after my companion called his son's name, the shifting vegetation quieted.

Soon, after a heralding of breaking sticks and crunching deadfall, another person stepped out of the undergrowth. Moving gingerly onto the trail, a twenty-something woman with multiple blue streaks in her blonde hair looked at us wild-eyed. "Please," she said, "I've lost my girlfriend. Can y'all help me?"

We explained our situation to her and exchanged timeframes. She claimed that she felt like she'd been searching for a couple days. But of course, it had only been a few hours.

"I only noticed how long I've been looking when I heard y'all's voices and checked the time on my phone," she said.

The woman compared phones with me, confirming that neither of us had a signal. The forty-something dad didn't have his phone, having given it to his son in case he got lost. Annoyed and embarrassed, he grumbled something about the boy's mother having an illogical aversion to technology and refusing to get him a phone of his own. Despite his misgivings, the concerned father still worriedly chided himself, "So much good it does him now."

I invited the blue-haired woman to join our posse and together, we continued searching. I was glad for her added company, I felt we had strength in numbers. We walked the trails single file, helping each other around pits of mud, a couple slippery switchbacks, and even a bizarre heap of centipedes, devouring the flesh of an animal skull in the middle of the path. At least, I hoped it was an animal skull. We continued alternating between names, calling for our friend, family and loved-one time after time. No matter our intensity or how many times we yelled, the woods remained silent.

I hastily checked my watch at one point to suddenly discover that somehow, over six hours had passed since I first started searching. It had been around four o'clock when I initially entered the woods and despite—maybe because—it being an overcast, gray day, there was no perceptible change in lighting. I asked my companions about this, both confirming that neither had lost any of the overcast daylight since beginning their own, frenzied searches. One claimed the late morning and the other the early afternoon, as the times when first they had come to the woods.

It turned out that my blue-haired companion had come to the woods with her girlfriend to propose to her. Reverentially, she told us of her love's vibrant passion for botany and how the woods were her girlfriend's early inspiration and favorite place to visit as a child.

"Especially in the morning," she said, smiling.

The thinning-haired man had brought his son to the woods for a good hike, since—in his opinion—the boy's mother didn't encourage him to play outside enough.

My lost friend had come to the woods with her dog, a mellow tempered, spotted foxhound, to work on her most recent project. She said she'd need at least an hour to take photos of several different mushroom species that she noticed during a previous visit. We made plans to watch the premiere of Disney's newest sci-fi show together that evening, so I agreed to wait the extra hour. After all, I had been anticipating the release of the show for over a year; at the time, I hadn't been stressed over waiting a little longer.

When four hours had passed, I began to worry. A call to her roommate informed me, "Yeah, as far as I know she's still in the woods," and that worry became dread.

We called out to our friend, our son and our hopefully, soon-to-be-betrothed's names. Nothing. After a few more yards our anxious group rounded a corner that faced a gradual angle up the hill. As the trail leveled out, the hill to our left became cliff-like; large parts of the slope were missing, as if chunked-out with an almighty ice cream scooper, allowing us to see the roots of the vegetation above poke out like accusing fingers. We called the names again and the woods began their loud conspiring once more. A little further down the path, in one of the clifflike alcoves on the trail's side, we found one of our lost ones.

"Liz!" Screamed the blue-haired woman. Her lost one was standing facing the dark, earthen cliff with her back to us and the trail. Her arms were raised, hands plunged into the tangled nest of vegetation on the cliff's short slope.

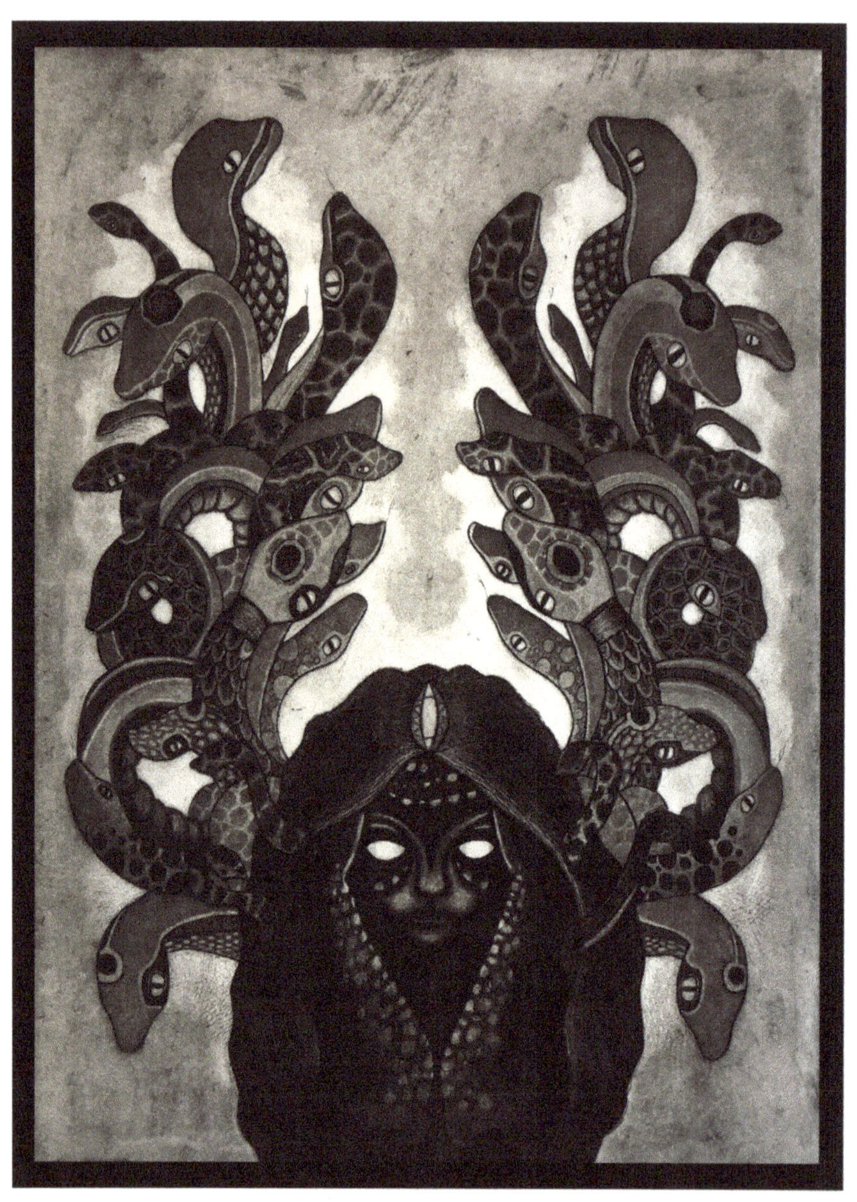

Medusa.

As we rushed forward, I distinctly saw the pale green, thorned roots wrapped around her forearms like grasping tentacles. They stretched up her arms in a spiral-pattern, seeming to throb in a sporadic, disturbing manner.

My blue-haired companion was at the enraptured woman's side, holding her shoulders, shaking her gently and saying, "Liz! Liz! Liz! Can you hear me?" Liz's head was tilted forward, her eyes squinted, a look of contented focus stretched across her face. Her lips moved as if she was murmuring something, but no words were audible.

"Liz!" Sobbed my blue-haired companion. She turned to us and begged, with tears streaming down her face, "Please, help me get her away from this."

The thinning-haired man and I approached and gingerly took hold of Liz's shoulders.

"Okay," said Liz's aspiring fiancé, "let's pull her back."

And so, we did. With surprising ease, the thorned, tentacle-like roots around her arms peeled away, exuding gentle streams of blood as they withered back into the hillside. We dragged a limp Liz back onto the trail, her rigidity gone as soon as the grasping roots were removed.

Liz swayed in the blue-haired woman's tight, panicked grasp, a small, white nub falling from her ear and into the mud, escaping our attention. Idly, she rubbed at her bloody forearms, blinked, and finally looked up at her tear-soaked girlfriend.

"Jade?" she asked absently, "Did you know the Himalayan blackberry grew this far north?"

Jade didn't have time to answer. With Liz's regaining of consciousness, the breathing of the woods intensified dramatically. The plants surrounding us throbbed with life once more. The intangible wind picked back up, the trees whispered loudly, and the foliage shook itself like a loosely mounted, antique motor. After a frightfully silent pause, the hillside Liz had been standing in front of, exploded. Dirt cascaded down to our feet on the trail as, what *had* been the thorned, rubbery roots grasping Liz came bursting forth. They had hardened, transforming into a myriad of long, spiked, boney legs belonging to verdantly bleached spiders that came surging out of the earth. The size of purse-dogs, the horrible, pale green arachnids scuttled viciously forward, angling their *click-clacking* bodies right for us. I screamed. Jade screamed. We all panicked.

"Run!" I bellowed, waving frantically at our frozen group. We did. We ran back the way we came, the whispering of the trees all around us and the scuttling of the spiders right behind. Liz's arms may have been bloody, but she was not weak; she and Jade led us down the path, the thinning-haired man following close behind.

It was only after a solid minute of panicked running that I dared to look back over my shoulder. The spiders had stopped. I could still see them, a dozen or so yards back, at the crest of the trail. Their coiling mass didn't seem to make any move towards us. They simply watched with their innumerable, beady eyes.

"Wait!" I called, "Stop for a moment." My group looked back, slowed and eventually halted in the middle of the trail.

"We shouldn't just wait for them to catch up," Jade declared, panting.

I shook my head emphatically, pointing at the spiders. "They aren't moving, let's just collect ourselves for a second."

"Maybe they wait for something else..." wondered the thinning-haired man. That idea gave us all pause and we stared at the distant, pale green arachnids for an imaginative moment.

Finally, Liz broke the silence. "What are we all looking at?" she asked, hesitantly casting her gaze from face to face in our small group. I was about to reply when resolutely, Liz's girlfriend spoke first.

"Nevermind that, we're leaving," Jade spat as she tugged on Liz's arm, careful not to touch her bleeding wounds. Despite it feeling like only a few minutes since we'd begun searching the woods together, the forty-eight hours Jade had supposedly spent in the woods suddenly became very clear in the lines of her face. She looked tired, hungry, and thirsty. Her lips were cracked, her eyes hooded.

"He and I still haven't found our lost ones though," I said worriedly, gesturing to the older man next to me. "Besides," I stammered, trying to think through the beating of my heart in my ears, "how do we know what Liz was doing at the hill isn't connected?"

"Connected?" asked Liz, squinting, "who even are you? Jade, who are these people?"

Jade shrugged and grunted again, "Later. I'll tell you later." She curtly told us she was sorry, but she wasn't going to wait any longer. She tugged on Liz's arm again and, like a tugboat slowly gaining momentum, they took off down the trail.

Liz looked back at us, her brow still furrowed, still powerless in Jade's wake. "Who the fu—" she said as they passed behind a tree and out of ear shot. Then there was just the two of us.

I looked back at the spiders, but they were gone. The wind and the whispering of the plant life had disappeared with them. The thinning-haired man met my eyes, my despair mirrored by his own. We stood in that spot for a moment, then wordlessly followed the trail in the direction Jade and Liz had gone. It was a solid few minutes before either of us spoke. I broke the silence first.

"I have a feeling that our lost ones won't be as deep in here as Liz was...the time they've been gone and all..." I trailed off, my conviction clearly wavering.

I was reassured by my companion muttering, "Yes, I can see that." Maybe he could, but there was little evidence to support the idea, just mild correlation. Still, we continued down the path.

Our pace had slowed since Jade and Liz left us. I do not know if my companion shared my line of thought—the couple disappeared before we could even discuss it—but finding Liz like she had been...wrist deep in spidery, thorned roots...Well, it made me fear how I'd possibly find my friend. If I found her at all.

After a few more yards, I was shaken from my dark reverie as I walked into the back of my companion. I shook myself back to awareness and looked to where he had directed his gaze.

We were in a flat section of the woods, a down sloping hill to our left, a wide, tree ringed meadow to our right. Behind a screen of wild rose bushes and sword ferns, a boy sat in the middle of the meadow, perhaps seven or eight years old. A neon blue windbreaker was laid at his side, discarded atop a splintered log and a shiny, rectangular phone gleamed from the jacket's surface. The boy held—what looked like—a black scorpion in his cupped palms.

The scorpion's body was nearly hidden by the boy's hands and its tail...its tail looked like a dark, bulbed tulip about to bloom. My thinning-haired companion evidently had the same difficulties of perception as he stammered, "What... what he is holding?" I saw his eyes widen in sudden, horrified realization. "Misha!" He screamed.

The boy looked up as his dad bolted forward. From the trail, I heard the boy say in a thin voice, "Dad! Look at this flower I picked."

It was then I noticed all the other 'flowers' around the boy. I yelled a warning to my companion. "Wait! The flowers! Wait!" The panicked father paid no heed, running off the trail towards his son, through the meadow of scorpions.

Their tails protruded from the ground, each looking like a curled, budded tulip with fat, sharply pointed bulbs. Hidden from view, their segmented bodies and pincered claws seemed to be buried under the debris of the forest floor but even still, I guessed there must've been hundreds of them. With a metallic clattering sound, the scorpions emerged from hiding as the man sprinted through them, yelling at his son to drop the venomous arachnid. Misha merely smiled at his father.

As the terrified dad approached, a large, dark scorpion sprang forward at the shambling man and managed to sink its bulbous stinger into his sweaty ankle. His determined, thunderous sprint did not waiver. The man bellowed in rage and pain and, reaching his son, he transferred that energy into a vicious swat at the scorpion curled in his son's palm. Amazingly, the docile arachnid hadn't stung the child.

The man, without slowing his gait, snatched up the kid and the discarded jacket in one fell swoop before angling away towards the general direction of the trailhead. He did not look back at me, he only ran with his son in his arms. The scorpions scuttled after him. The father and son, and the pursuing pincered swarm, disappeared into the brush.

It all happened so quickly, I hadn't known what to do to help. Now, I didn't know what to do with myself. The bulbous, black scorpions hadn't come in my direction. The pale green spiders were nowhere to be seen. I wasn't motivated to run, so I walked. I walked back in the direction I had come, indirectly following my former companions and their recovered lost ones. Where was my lost one? Where was my friend?

I didn't call her name anymore, fearful of what people or creatures it might summon from the undergrowth. Selfishly, I was stressed at the idea of more people appearing with lost ones of their own to distract me from my search.

I was terrified of what other creepy-crawlies would chase after me. However, my paranoia didn't have long to fester. Only a dozen or so yards past the venomous meadow, I saw a flash through the trees.

It wasn't bright, but it was enough to grab my attention. It was a camera flash; I was sure of it. I paused, waited, and the flash came again. I called my friend's name, managing to push aside my anxieties momentarily.

"Holly!" I yelled. The whispering of the woods grew louder. The flash came again. "Holly!" I again called and stepped off the path. The woods that merely whispered before began to shout as I moved away from the trail. The trees passed secrets to each other, loudly conspiring against me, debating what to do with this disruptive humanoid in their midst. I began to jog as the flashes came quicker. The trees grew louder. I started running, the flashes seeming to come in time to my desperate exhalations. The wind intensified again, and as it did, branches from the canopy above began to drop, hissing through the air as they streamed past my head.

"Holly!" I screamed as I ran. The flashes weren't any closer. A falling branch hit me on the shoulder, but it didn't feel like a branch. It wasn't rigid and brittle, it was soft and flexible, trying to coil itself around my neck before sliding off. It hissed again.

I didn't slow down. I couldn't slow down, as somewhere in the back of my head I realized these were not dead branches at all, but heavy, very much alive *snakes*. Green as the moss on the trees, the snakes dropped from the canopy, attempting to gain purchase on my shoulders, my head, my neck. Their collective hissing added to the cacophony of the woods, nearly drowning out my scream for my friend. "Holly!"

Finally, the flashing did get a little closer. I could swear it was coming from behind the next bank of trees, only a few seconds away. The thunderous, deafening rustling of the trees grew louder still, splitting the grey, overcast day with a creaking, animalistic roar. "*Aarrff*," howled the wind.

Then, as I nearly tripped on an exposed root, one of the snakes got me. It dropped heavily onto my shoulders, coiling itself around my neck. It hissed in my ear, then sank its fangs right into the flesh above my jacket collar. I screamed and nearly fell. The snake slid off: its mission accomplished. It seemed to hiss with pleasure as I staggered on. My neck was warm, my body tingling with pins and needles as if every one of my limbs had suddenly fallen asleep. The pain was unbearable.

The flash came again, right behind the large cedar before me. I stumbled towards it. No more snakes fell. The trees had stopped their arguing.

"Holly," I moaned. The flashing paused, the silence of the trees filling the void momentarily before a sharp dog's bark split the sudden stillness. "*Aarrff!*"

"Douglas?" Quickly followed a reply. I rounded the cedar tree and there she was, Holly, with her vintage camera, taking pictures of fungi growing on the ground around the cedar's roots. Her brown and white spotted dog leapt in the air excitedly, leashed to a decomposing stump a few feet behind her owner. "*Aarrff!*" it loudly yelped again, pulling its lips back in an awkward smile.

"Holly...thank God," I said weakly, before practically collapsing in her arms.

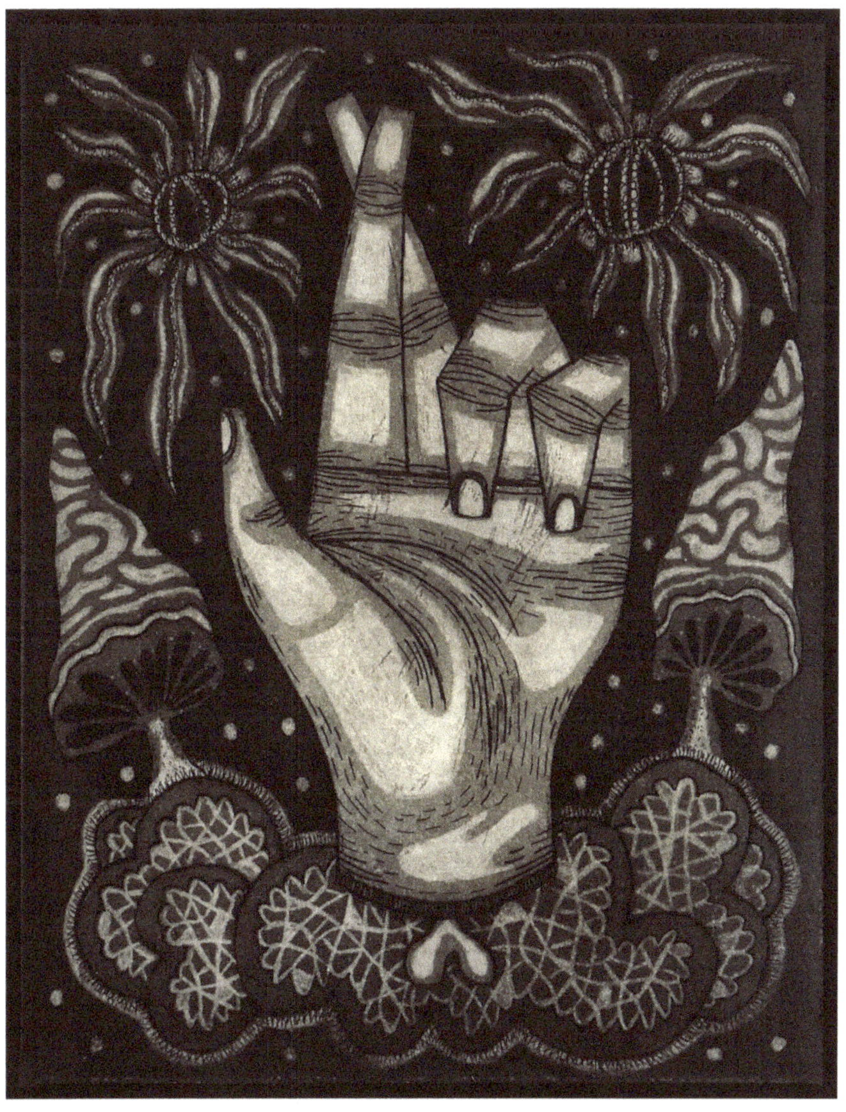

Fingers Crossed.

"Jesus Christ Douglas, you look like shit. Why are you covered in sweat and...bark?"

I tried to gesture behind me, to explain the snakes and scorpions and spiders, but all I could manage was to feebly ask to leave, to get out of the woods. Holly looked at me puzzled but, seeing the fear and panic in my eyes, sternly nodded. She packed away her camera in her shoulder bag, snatched up her dog's leash and helped me to my feet. I hadn't realized I had been kneeling in the dirt.

"Okay Douglas," she said worriedly, "let's get back to the main trail. It's easy to get lost in here."

We made our way back to the beaten path, going slowly thanks to my rubbery legs. Holly helped me step over several fallen moss-covered branches that my tired feet tripped on as we negotiated the bumpy, forested trail.

We walked mostly in silence, although Holly did ask a few questions. Namely, what I was doing in the woods in the first place. I told her I was worried after she didn't show up and that I thought she might've been lost. She apologized and casually explained she hadn't had any choice, that despite going on a hike to the wood's highest peak, she hadn't been able to get a signal on her phone.

"Otherwise," she promised me, "I would have totally let you know I needed to postpone. I just found too many perfect fungal subjects at full maturity today. I couldn't risk a frost ruining all the examples I found for my catalogue, you know?"

We passed by the mud pits on the trail, helping each other across. Holly had to pull her dog out of the sodden earth, scolding her for rolling in the dirt. "I just gave you a bath yesterday dammit," she sighed, tiredly. We passed the animal skull the centipedes had previously feasted upon. The carnivorous arthropods were gone. It was a deer skull after all.

Pulling the dog away from the skull, Holly asked me offhandedly, "Did you take your meds today?"

I nodded hesitantly in response and murmured to her down-jacketed back, "Yes." But I did not elaborate. I did not tell her that I was lying. I did not tell her that my worry earlier that day had caused me to forget. I was supposed to take them with lunch, but the meal and my medication escaped my attention as the hours of anxiety stretched on, as I stressed over my friend being lost in the woods.

"Good," Holly cheerfully said, "now let's go watch that premiere."

We were nearing the trailhead when Holly had me wait for a moment as she ducked behind a tree and dragged her bike out from its hiding place. I rubbed at my neck, reminded that she was always cautious of her bike being stolen. I winced as my hand brushed against a bruise forming right above my jacket collar.

Holly pushed her Santa Cruz by its handlebars, her dog happily padding along beside us. I berated myself for letting the waves of stress and anxiety get the better of me. The woods and all its mysteries remained silent as we left its depths; there were no whispers of farewell.

At the trailhead, we were greeted by the flashing lights of a county ambulance and two parked cars on the far side of the road. I suppose they had escaped my attention in my rushed, single-minded entrance into the woods earlier that day.

I saw my former companions seated in the open back of the ambulance, being tended to by two EMTs. The thinning-haired man had a juice box and bag of cashews and was diligently downing both by the mouthful. The EMTs were chiding him about needing to prepare better for long hikes.

"I mean really, Mr. Ilionov," said the female EMT, "being diabetic you should know better. You're lucky that your twisted ankle isn't worse than it is. You're even luckier that your son called us when he did."

Misha stood next to his father, worrying at a dark tulip bulb in his small hands. Liz was next to the male EMT, being handed a small bottle of Neosporin for her forearms that were marred only by the slightest scrapes and scratches a blackberry bush could deal out. Her free hand fidgeted with a single, white Air Pod between her fingers. The previously unnoticed Subaru across the street honked its horn and I noticed Jade sitting impatiently in the driver seat.

The male EMT spotted Holly and me then and called out across the gravel lot, "Hey, are you two okay? Do you need any help?"

Holly responded, "I'm fine but my friend might, he got himself kinda lost in there."

Wearily, I waved them off. "I'm good, just tired," I had no desire to explain my psychosomatic adventure to anyone.

"Well, be sure to hydrate," said the female EMT, "or you'll need an ambulance too."

The thinning-haired father sheepishly smiled and pulled his son close.

Holly mounted her bike and I grabbed mine from where I had left it. I hadn't thought to lock it, yet another detail that escaped my mind when I first entered the woods. Holly's dog sat expectantly next to her owner, her wagging tail sweeping gusts of gravel dust side to side. I mounted my bike beside Holly and, as we began to pedal through the overcast afternoon, checked the time. I had convinced myself that I spent all day in the woods, but of course, that had been a worried exaggeration. It was a quarter to five, as we left the rural, trailhead road, together.

THE MAPMAKER

Words: Benjamin Kessler Art: Charlie Salas-Humara

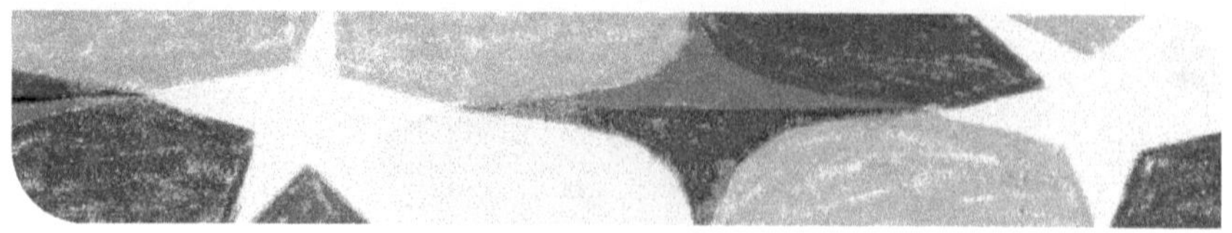

Benjamin Kessler's (he/him) work has appeared in *Bellevue Literary Review, Hobart, DIAGRAM, Pithead Chapel, Entropy,* and more. He currently lives in Portland, Oregon.

Charlie Salas-Humara (he/him) creates his paintings as representations of the "in between spaces" of the world at view. Placing equal emphasis on the negative and on the active elements of his canvases, he questions how much we see when observing an object and how much we see when attempting to see through it. Rough outlines, isolated letters, smudged shapes and symbols have us tugging at an understanding of works with such titles as *Riford Road* or *Calumet*. In his own words, Salas-Humara is building the "alleys, hidden tufts of foliage, and clandestine doorways" of his childhood in such a manner that the many layers of lines, colors, and transformations contort as much as they reveal about his alternate world.

The mapmaker maps the anatomy of our kitchen cupboards, the geography of every plate and stemless wine glass, the hardwater whorls in our shallow sink. He maps the alignment of the furniture, the migrant divots left in the rug from us pushing out and pulling in the sharp-cornered coffee table. He charts patterns of wear on the couch cushions, hot spots/cold spots, the erosion of the buttons on the TV remote, the channels we skip and the ones upon which we linger. He maps the scratches on the melamine end table, the contour lines around chocolate rings left by cups without coasters. So too he details the coasters, their movement around the apartment—the windowsill near the wingback chair, the empty bookshelf rung, off-center on the dining room table. One was missing, now two. He maps the way the sheets crumple and crease, how lacquer wears away off the headboard, canals through dust from fingertips adjusting the lampshade. He catalogs stains and lint and the pilling of the mattress pad. The mapmaker maps where the sweat pools and the hands press and hair overhangs. The mapmaker maps patterns. Patterns in space and in time. Temporal. Spatial. Songbirds. Treebirds, streetbirds, beachbirds. Plovers, sandpipers, killdeer, whimbrels, oystercatchers, surfbirds, and long-billed dowitchers. He maps when there are no birds as well.

And I love the mapmaker.

In the evenings the mapmaker and I watch television, we take turns stirring the sauce so it doesn't burn. We play rummy five-hundred at home and darts when we go out. We once drove to the Grand Canyon and the mapmaker took so many pictures.

When we married, the mapmaker worked at the utility company, tracing buried power lines on a computer screen minute by minute, day after day. Now, though, he doesn't work. Now, he maps. While I occupy the couch, flicking through internet ads I am to proofread and optimize, the mapmaker ventures out. The mapmaker calls these excursions "recon." On recon the mapmaker takes with him two soft-lead pencils, a pocket notebook, a point-and-shoot camera, and a sweat-soaked baseball hat through which the plastic skeleton of the bill peeks out between frayed patches. When he returns at the end of the day he leaves his notebook in the alcove near the door which at one point housed a rotary telephone. While he showers I pore over what he has seen, what he deems worthy of record.

The mapmaker maps movement, maps stillness, maps time and energy, maps the best houses to get candy at on Halloween, maps Jewish houses, Mexican houses, Italian houses, red fire hydrants, yellow fire hydrants, which houses still get a newspaper, which houses leave their garbage cans out days after pickup, gas prices, where the best sled hills are, the slapdash bicycle ramps, the crumbling tree forts, maps where men are bald and women freckled.

The mapmaker says that within the city exist infinite unique geographies.

When it is time for bed I tell the mapmaker I love him and he says I love you too then he goes to make maps. That's what mapmakers do.

Last week the mapmaker's mother visited our apartment. She had not told us she was coming. She wanted to talk to her son, and I gave them the privacy the severity of her request implied by going out and cleaning the already spotless car. Of what little conversation I caught upon leaving I determined something was wrong with the mapmaker's younger brother.

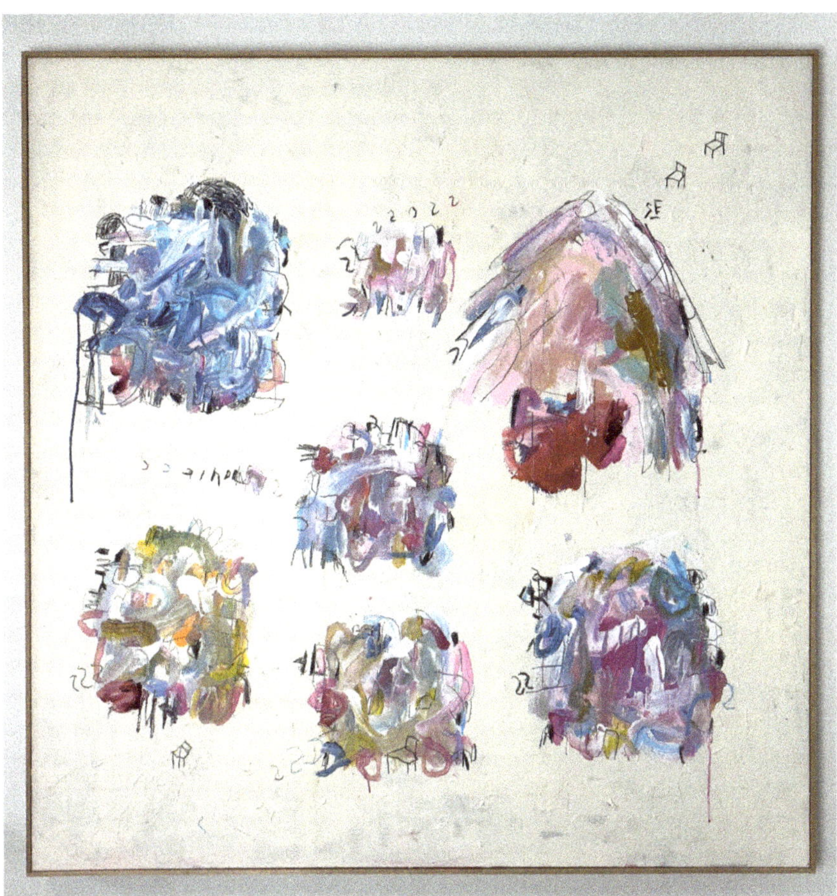

Since that day the mapmaker has gone out on recon less and less, and now he spends the entirety of his day in the guest bedroom, emerging only to use the restroom and take toasted sandwiches back with him from the kitchen. During this time his presence is only announced by light flaking out from around the doorjamb and the occasional ripple of paper tearing from the spiral coil of his sketchpad.

We still spend time with one another in the evening, yes-anding over cooking competition shows and passing the crossword puzzle between us when a difficult clue appears, but the mapmaker lacks a certain something, as though a plug has been pulled and whatever had fueled him before is slowly draining out. We've stopped having sex; we've stopped going out to eat; we've stopped discovering in one another the things that once energized our relationship.

Every so often I feel compelled to ask the mapmaker more about what his mother told him, but I decide that it is his knowledge to broadcast, and that to pull it out of him would perhaps further unseat the hinges that hold him together.

So I give the mapmaker his space, and during the day scroll and scroll through photos of products enriching the lives of happy families through their apparent usefulness, slashing through filler words in copy so as to make the point with haste.

Though one day I am given no choice but to insert myself into the mapmaker's private moments. Medication of his arrives via UPS and he is required to sign for it. I knock quietly, then firmly after I get no response, and then allow myself into the guest room, the walls of which have been papered over with intricate sketchbook scribblings. Every last space is covered with the mapmaker's handiwork. Even the windows are obscured, the light through the paper giving the space a sepia tone as though it is some flashback I am experiencing.

And the mapmaker is gone. Given my station in the living room I would have seen him should he have gone anywhere. It is as though he has vanished.

I tell the delivery man that the mapmaker is not here and he responds that he can wait. I tell him no, that he should leave, that he would be wasting his time waiting, which I don't know is true or not. I half-expect the mapmaker to pop out at any moment from behind a half-closed door and wrap his arms around me in his familiar way but it doesn't happen.

After the delivery person leaves I return to the guest room and examine what the mapmaker has made. Black ink lines, like those from a standard rollerball, are layered neatly on the paper, forming grids and coming together in shapes that resemble trees and houses if their resolution had been heavily decreased.

They are maps. Though of what, I am not sure.

I turn to leave but then see the lines on one of the maps begin to move. The ink on this particular sheet of paper is fresh enough that it smears slightly as I run my fingers over it, imprinting itself on my skin. A series of trailing hash marks stumbles across the page, appearing one by one in a meandering line like footprints in snow. I follow the trail as it navigates the page, watch carefully as it stops and starts, crosses over on itself, retraces a route multiple times.

I exit the room, closing the door behind me, and thoroughly search the rest of the apartment for any trace of the mapmaker, even going so far as to look under our bed. When I find no trace of him, and the myriad calls to his cell phone return nothing but an inactive voicemail box, I take my place back on the couch and half-read celebrity gossip until, as the sun slants through our back window, the mapmaker emerges from the guest room and sits beside me as though nothing at all mysterious has happened, after which we eat reheated Thai food and talk about a mutual friend's recent divorce.

The next day I again go into the guest room, and again watch as a series of consecutive hash marks, like a stutter across the page, make their way through one of the hand drawn maps. I watch the motion for a good while longer this time, missing a meeting at work in the process, and notice that at times the markings migrate to an entirely new map, disappearing and reappearing on the other side of the room.

As days go on I begin a routine of logging into my computer to erect a facade that I am indeed working, but in reality I spend my entire day in the guest room watching the trails trace themselves across the pages. I eat my lunch standing up in front of them, swipe at my phone when the figure moving through the maps stops and lingers in one place in particular. I bring in a chair and return it to the dining room before the mapmaker returns from wherever he spends his days. I cancel lunch date plans with girlfriends and allow episodes of *Jeopardy*! to accumulate on my DVR.

One day the mapmaker's father phones and the mapmaker takes the call in our bedroom, alone. Before I can stop myself my ear is pressed against the bedroom door, and I eavesdrop that the mapmaker's brother has taken up with some unsavory people and has disappeared. When the mapmaker comes back to the living room he does so in complete silence, tossing his phone into a pile of cushions on the couch. He does not speak for the rest of the evening and I do not press. We watch World Series highlights on television, wash the dishes together, and then go to sleep. In bed, barely hanging on to consciousness, I tell the mapmaker that I love him very much, to which he responds by nestling his body closer to mine.

When I wake in the morning the mapmaker is not in bed beside me. His dresser drawers have been taken out and upturned and mostly emptied. A photo of the two of us in front of the *Welcome to Fabulous Las Vegas* is gone as are the mapmaker's wallet and the multitool I had given him the previous Christmas.

Still in my pajamas I go immediately to the guest room and find a note taped to the door with my name written on it. I pull it down and read and reread it, fingering the fold in the paper creased by the mapmaker's hand. He knew that it was here that I would first go looking for him. Perhaps he knew that I had been spending my days inside the guest room, had known from the beginning.

I ease the door open and search for movement, eventually finding the string of marks on a map freshly drawn. I hold the note tight between my hands as though it were a map I am following myself, one that has led me to this exact place. The marks march rhythmically forward until they hit the edge of the paper, beside which is a square of newly unobscured wall still bright with white primer. I spin, looking for where the path has continued, but find nothing.

I think for a moment that I should enter the map myself, follow the mapmaker's trail and discover the artifacts of his pathfinding: a campfire gone to cinders, footprints in baked mud, an assemblage of snack cake wrappers piled atop a stone. Though unlike the mapmaker I would have no intuition to interpret these signposts. I would wander and lose myself, something he would not have wanted.

I stare at the empty space where the marks end and wonder if he knows the way back, if he even cares.

PARTY DOGS

I can't help
but imagine
what comes next
after I'm gone
snorting sod in my sleep
a heavy thing in my hand
something to fall to the floor & wake me
these dreams are worth recording
the birds are safe in the leaves
dappled camo shadow nest
I believe we are visited by wild animals
and sidewalk cats
and party dogs
when we need them
I believe in reading my lines
when I don't know what to say
I have a messy book with too many flags
bookmarks and dog ears
sometimes it is too late to respond
the joke doesn't come
until you're in the shower unarmed
defaulting
to a grey screen
truly pixels of white and black snow

Nathan Wade Carter (he/him) is a queer, grey-a, non-binary poet, musician, and artist living in Portland, Oregon. He is the editor and founder of *SUSAN / The Journal*. Nathan also writes and performs songs under the name Purrbot. Find him online at nathanwadecarter.com, and check out his chapbook, *ROYGBIV* (Ursus Americanus Press 2017).

JULY 5TH

my desire is an ant
so
seems small
but is connected to all the other little bits of want
building a nest and a hill
a labyrinth map of how to get to me
in some ways so easy
it is the web of ways
that is called love or just feeling
and when you get to the end there is another door
and the concept of destination is buried and flooded over
I clutch at the minotaur's strong arm
as a remora to a shark
as a leaf on a hedge
no one
noticed
on its own
so
my point
I am not fireworks exploding
but I am us standing around beforehand
and after
I am colorful wrapping
containing
I am lighter
lightning
I am long match
I am asphalt ash
I am July 5th

EITHER (FOR *OR ELLIOTT)*

Words: Erik Grove

Art: Jessie Weitzel Le Grand

(Photos By: Mario Gallucci)

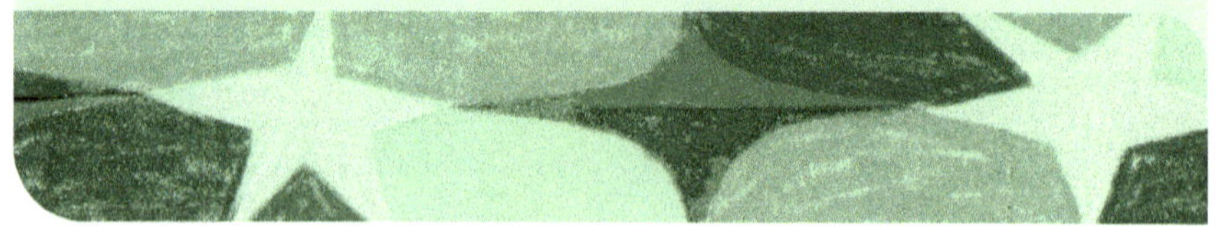

Erik Grove (he/him) is a writer, long distance runner, and little dog wrangler doing things in Portland, OR. He enjoys tacos, robots, and using italics for *emphasis*. He is a current Bad Dream Factory Worker studying fiction and mischief with mentors Chuck Palahniuk and Chelsea Cain. He is a guest host of the Overcast speculative fiction podcast and you can find his work in the *SPACE COCAINE* anthology series and upcoming in *ESCAPE POD*. Find him at his webpage **www.erikgrove.com** or on Twitter **@erikgrove** where he occasionally tweets dog photos, marathon training nonsense, and sundry writerly shenanigans.

Jessie Weitzel Le Grand's (she/her) work presents objects from imagined alternate realities connected to our own. Jessie holds a BFA from Pacific Northwest College of Art, an MAT from Marylhurst University and has exhibited work recently at Lefebvre & Fils (Paris, France), Outback Arthouse (Los Angeles), Oregon Contemporary (Portland, OR) and Lazy Oaf's "Take a Break" in London. Jessie is a co-founder of Carnation Contemporary and Well Well Projects. She teaches second grade in Portland, OR. She is currently thinking about inner-worlds, unsolved mysteries, and conscious plants. And video games.

Instagram: **@_ny_by**
Website: **jessieweitzel.com**

Elliott Smith, Portlandish singer-songwriter born August 6th, 1969 and deceased October 21st, 2003 came back from the dead in the Most Fun Place on Earth. He was first noticed loitering by the butterfly carousel, eyeing the pony-sized technicolor insects and their adolescent sticky-fingered riders with curious suspicion. Park security officers, dressed in pink fuzzy kitty kitty costumes to avoid alarming the patrons, cornered him by the bubble waterfall. Before Elliott could ask any questions or sing any songs, they hit him with tasers.

"We have an aberration," the pink fuzzy kitty kitty in charge reported on his security radio.

The orders came quickly and followed the playbook. The Most Fun Place on Earth did practice drills for this sort of thing: create a perimeter; take him to Guest Services; deploy a jaunty old timey parade with a few of those people that walk on very tall stilt legs; free waffle churro fries for everyone; call Quality Assurance.

After the call to Quality Assurance a case manager was assigned; Elijah Bennington-Bird, a senior case manager and serious man of average height who gave the impression of someone much taller. He acted quickly to resolve the situation and minimize social media uproar. His first decision was to include sticky-sweet dipping sauce with the free waffle churro fries because, he surmised, people were less likely to tweet about the Elliott Smith situation if their fingers were covered in cinnamon sugar and sticky-sweet dipping sauce.

Elijah Bennington-Bird's second decision was to call an all hands meeting in the Hall of Imagination.

"This is a volatile situation," Elijah Bennington-Bird told the gathered imaginonauts. He stood behind a narrow podium in front of a screen that showed Elliott Smith pacing around a white room.

"We can't have *that man* spontaneously apparating in Wonder Town. There could be *birthday parties*."

"Hello?" Elliott Smith called out. "What, uh, what's going on?" He looked down at his shoes. "And why did you take my shoelaces?"

A murmur moved through the Hall of Imagination.

Elijah Bennington-Bird muted Elliott Smith. "Whoever is responsible for this, we will find out. Step forward and take responsibility."

Patrick Neary, a rank II imaginonaut with an inoffensive bushy mustache and a Wish Bear Care Bear belly badge tattoo on his stomach winced. "Shit," he whispered to himself. Elliott Smith was his fault. It wasn't intentional but these things never are. He was supposed to be making clouds that looked like otters but instead he made an early 21st century sad man. Reluctantly, he raised his hand.

Elijah Bennington-Bird narrowed his eyes like a vulture that seemed taller than he actually was. "My office," he snarled and curled his finger into a shape that looked exactly like his voice sounded. "Now."

"Well, you're getting fired," one of Patrick's fellow imaginonauts, Lara Rojas, a rank III in the happy earworm song department and a collector of unexpected socks told him.

"Everyone's slipped," Patrick replied and looked at his fellow imaginonauts. "I mean, a little bit... Right?"

Lester Munson, rank III whimsy, recoiled, personally offended by the suggestion.

His face turned red and then white and then redder.

Lara Rojas smiled cheerily. "If you really beg for it, maybe you'll get health insurance through next month."

Patrick didn't think that was very likely.

***

Elijah Bennington-Bird's office was not fun or happy or pleasant. His desk was severe. His walls were aggressively undecorated. He looked at Patrick with fingers templed in front of his mouth, nostrils flaring with each deliberate and accusatory breath. He chose his words carefully and delivered them in a stern and measured cadence.

"How did this happen?"

"I was on clouds, you know," Patrick said. "And I guess I sort of... wandered."

Elijah Bennington-Bird looked from Patrick to a computer screen. "Your media consumption and behavioral analysis are all within parameters. There is nothing to indicate an *Elliott Smith.*"

"No, I, uh, I get that. I haven't thought about Elliott Smith in years. Years and years," Patrick recalled.

"And?"

"And I was doing the clouds and this guy I work with, Anish, he had this smirk on his face and it made me think about Casey Affleck."

"Casey Affleck is *not* approved either."

"I know, I know. I didn't want to think about Casey Affleck but I saw Anish smirking then like, all at once I thought about that scene in *Good Will Hunting* when Casey Affleck gets in the front seat of the car after Matt Damon leaves to go find a girl in the end. Casey doesn't really smirk, I guess. It's sort of a Casey Affleck micro smirk. Do you know what I mean?"

Elijah Bennington-Bird's nostrils flared three times in silence before he answered: "I have not seen *Good Will Hunting.*"

"Really? Well, I just ruined the ending a little bit."

Elijah Bennington-Bird clapped his hands. "Elliott Smith," he said to get them back on topic.

"Sure. Well, Elliott Smith had a bunch of songs on the soundtrack. It went from Anish to Casey Affleck to *Good Will Hunting* and then I guess... I brought Elliott Smith back to life in the amusement park."

"This isn't good," Elijah Bennington-Bird stated. "This man is... maudlin."

"Yeah."

"There are certain associations with narcotics and behavioral abnormalities."

"Sure."

"It prompts questions no one wants to answer."

"It's not ideal," Patrick agreed. "But how long can he last?"

Elijah Bennington-Bird's eyes widened. "*Last?*" he repeated.

"Right. How long until he just... goes away? He'll just mumble on back to Wes Anderson Heaven or wherever Elliott Smiths go sooner or later."

Elijah Bennington-Bird's lips slid up and back revealing, impossibly, every single perfectly straight tooth in his mouth. "Are you mentally deficient?"

Patrick thought about how to answer. He thought about keeping his health insurance for another month. "...maybe?"

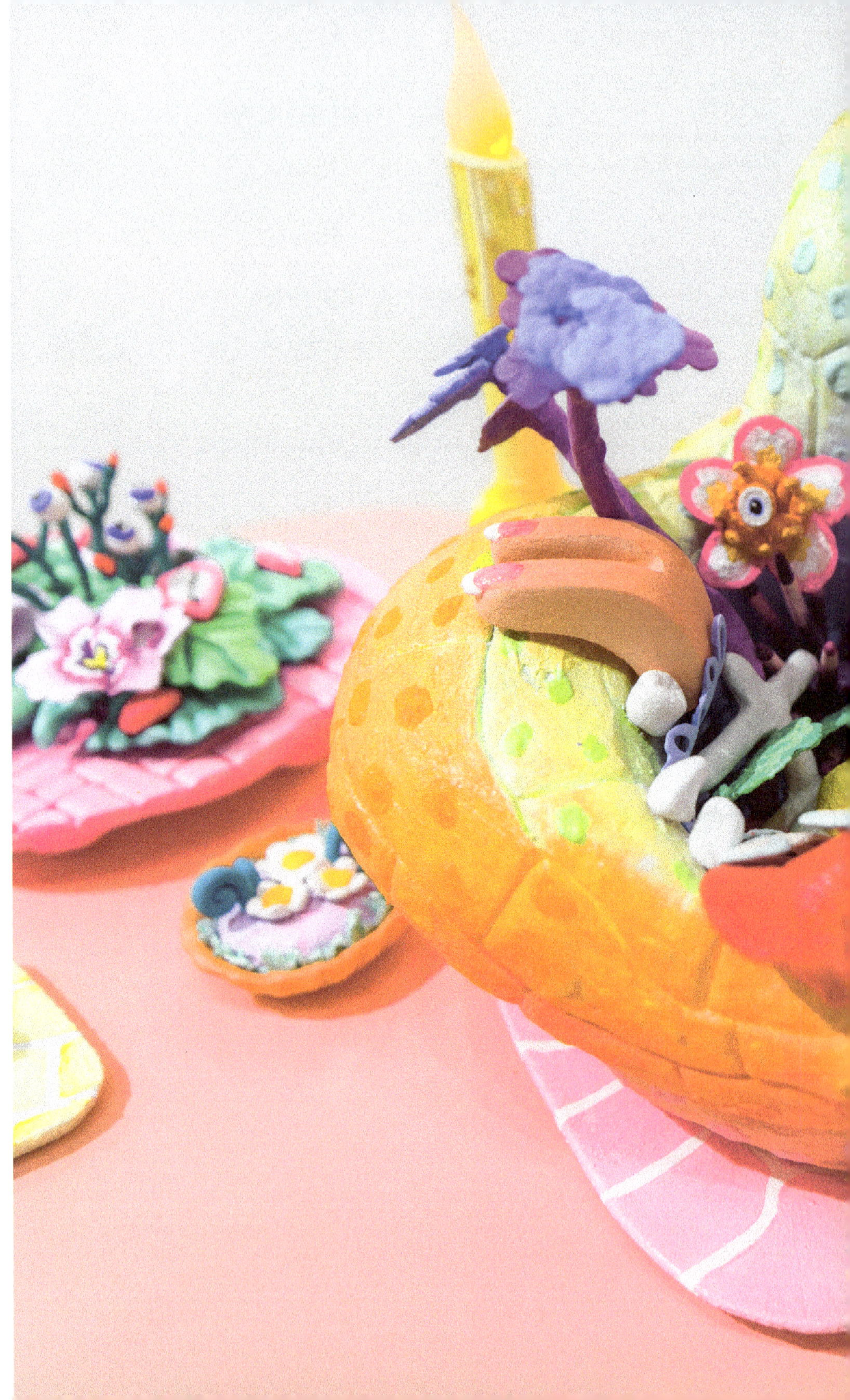

Pupil Blooms.

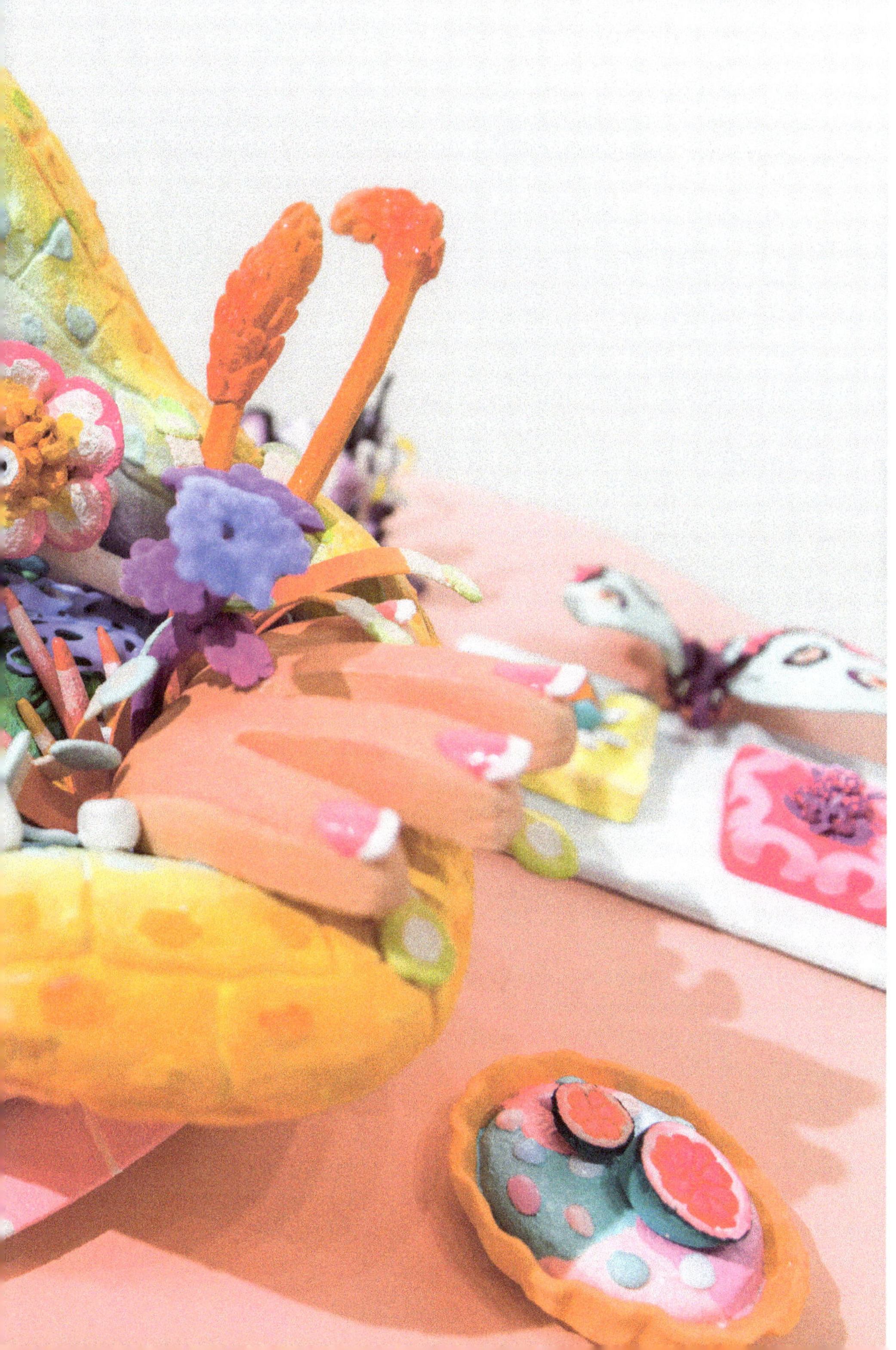

"The technology that powers the Hall of Imagination is incredibly sophisticated Mr. Neary, far more sophisticated than you seem to realize."

Patrick nodded. "Right on."

"The machines that reach into your brain and give form and life to your mentally deficient thoughts do not make things that just *go away sooner or later.* Elliott Smith is here now. He's in the office next door." Elijah Bennington-Bird pointed to the wall to his left. "And he's not going anyway."

"Wow." Patrick was stunned by the implications of this and perplexed that the long-term nature of creating Elliott Smiths had not been covered in the on-boarding materials. "I feel like we should be using this technology to make sandwiches and clean water instead of neon glitter fairies and park benches made out of cupcakes." Patrick saw the naked corporate fury seething from between Elijah Bennington-Bird's teeth. "But I guess that wouldn't sell as many tickets."

"This is the Most Fucking Fun Place on the Fucking Earth, Mr. Neary, do you fucking understand me, you mentally deficient stutter fuck?"

"...maybe?"

Elijah Bennington-Bird tugged on the vest of his tight vertically striped suit, jostled in is seat and hissed. "Then you understand what must be done?"

Patrick nodded. "I..." he shook his head. "No."

Elijah Bennington-Bird opened the drawer of his desk and produced a handgun.

"Wait. Are you...?" Patrick blinked. "Are you kidding me right now?"

"Do I *look* like I'm kidding you right now?"

Elijah Bennington-Bird did *not.*

***

Technically as long as Elliott Smith was murdered by the imaginonaut who created him within park bounds it was, legally, considered editing and the Most Fun Place on Earth Corporation would not be liable in any way.

"It's a loophole," Elijah Bennington-Bird told Patrick. "Our lawyers assure me that it will not be legally difficult for you. I suggest you shoot him twice in the head. Double-tap." Elijah Bennington-Bird knocked on the desk twice in rapid succession. "To be thorough."

Patrick held the gun. It weighed much more than he ever imagined a gun would weigh. The heaviness of the gun made him feel weak. "You want me to go next door and..."

"No. Not in the building. The janitorial union has strict rules about where they will and will not dispose of remains and miscellaneous debris."

"Sure," Patrick said. "...do I take him to the food court then?"

"After the jaunty old timey parade I had Wonder Town closed for maintenance. Take him there."

Patrick stared at the gun. "And after I... what, um, what's my employment situation?"

"Oh, you will be terminated immediately. But if you do this, you'll be given three months' severance."

"And health insurance?"

Elijah Bennington-Bird nodded. "And health insurance."

Patrick's doctor had been very clear that it was important that he not skip doses of his antidepressants in order to sustain the therapeutic effects. It also seemed like after executing Elliott Smith in Wonder Town would be a particularly bad time to stop taking his medication. That was the sort of event that could trigger what his doctor would call a therapeutic setback.

"No one's going to see?"

"Every single person employed by the Most Fun Place on Earth Corporation is under a strict NDA to never reveal anything about any murders that may or may not occur within the park."

Patrick did not recall signing such an NDA but he had signed a lot of things. There was a lot of paperwork during orientation. It occurred to him that the Most Fun Place on Earth Corporation might have a proprietary stake in his dreams in perpetuity.

Elijah Bennington-Bird opened the drawer in his desk again and produced a t-shirt. "Should you get... miscellaneous debris on your shirt."

Patrick accepted the shirt. "Thanks," he said and then realized it wasn't his size. His smile turned to a frown. Elijah Bennington-Bird grinned. He *knew* it wasn't Patrick's size. Of course that vulture fucker knew.

With the handgun and the t-shirt Patrick went next door to introduce himself to Elliott Smith.

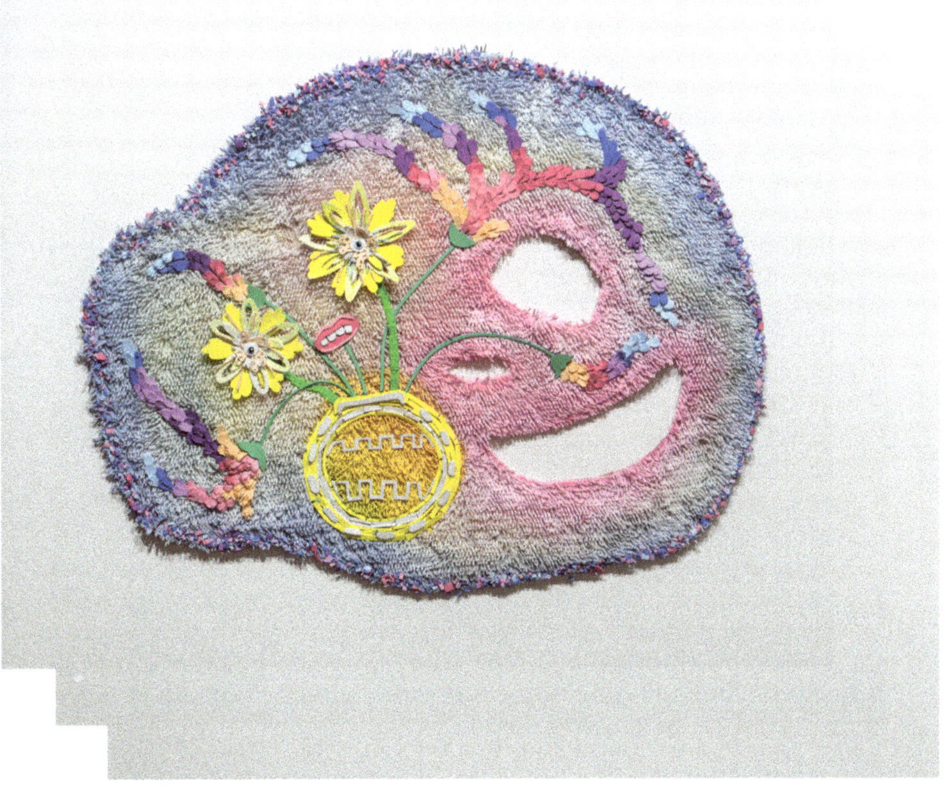

Limbo Lounge Shag #1.

"Hi," he said. "How you doing?"

Elliott was sitting on the floor. "Confused." He spoke softly, calmly. He didn't make eye contact but instead looked off to the side.

"What do you remember exactly?"

"Exactly... very little. It's... Jumbled."

One of the things Elijah Bennington-Bird explained was that Elliott Smith wasn't Elliott Smith. Or more specifically he was but he wasn't. He was Patrick's imagined version of Elliott Smith. The Elliott Smith he vaguely recalled hearing on the stereo in the background when he was in high school and recognized on indie movie soundtracks. He didn't have Elliott Smith's memories or experiences. He wasn't an Elliott Smith zombie or ghost. He was a poster on someone's wall. A cautionary tale.

"He might actually have some of your memories," Elijah Bennington-Bird had said. "He's a part of you. A deep manifestation of some elements of yourself. So really, you'll just be shooting a part of yourself in the head."

"Twice," Patrick added. To be thorough.

Patrick thought about what parts of himself Elliott Smith embodied and then he thought about Elijah Bennington-Bird's double-tap knock. The whole situation was really going to dominate his counseling sessions for a little while. Four sessions, at least.

"Can I get you anything?"

Elliott looked up at Patrick for the first time. "Can I have my shoelaces?"

"I can ask about that."

Elliott nodded and reached into the pocket of his black jeans. "Cigarettes."

"Sure. And some kind of fire making thing, right?"

Elliott nodded slowly. "Yeah. And also, do you have anything to eat or...?"

"Like a sandwich?"

A wrinkle of a smile appeared on the dead singer-songwriter's face.

Patrick shook his head. "But there aren't any sandwiches. It's fucked up. There *should* be. There really should be."

"Oh."

"Do you like cupcakes?"

Elliott stood up. "Okay."

"I don't have them with me," Patrick clarified. "I can take you to them." In Wonder Town, he thought. Where I'm going to execute you.

Elliott didn't respond but waited patiently for Patrick's next move.

Patrick snapped his fingers. "I'll work on the cigarettes and fire maker. I'll be right back."

"And shoelaces. Please."

Patrick winked at his manifestation and backed out of the door before he started hyperventilating in the hall. He stumbled into the bathroom and got sick in the sink. He ran the water and watched it wash everything away. He looked up at his reflection. He never imagined he would be luring an Academy Award nominated musician into a theme park with confections so he could legally blow his brains out. No. It was going to take more like 40 sessions with his counselor for this.

***

In the employee lounge Patrick found cigarettes and a lighter. He took them back to Elliott Smith triumphantly.

"No shoelaces, huh?"

"Shit. No. They were all out."

"Am I kidnapped or something?"

Patrick shook his head nervously. "Of course not. Why would you think that? Did someone tell you that? Look, let's just hurry up and get you some cupcakes! They have sprinkles."

Elliott Smith was surprisingly trusting and followed Patrick out of the Hall of Imagination without any further questions vis-à-vis his potential abduction. Good. It was good that Patrick didn't have to say things out loud.

When they got outside the sun was shining and it smelled like bubblegum. The sun was always shining and it always smelled like bubblegum in the Most Fucking Fun Place on Earth.

Elliott tilted his face up toward the sun and took a contented breath. "It's nice."

Patrick had never seen the park empty and quiet like this. He knew that there were thousands of candy-lipped jumped-up Ritalin monsters in Pegasus Park and Giggleburg but Wonder Town was almost tranquil.

Elliott squinted his eyes. "Are we in Disn—?"

"No," Patrick interrupted. "Absolutely not. There are clear differences and the copyright offices are quite diligent about that sort of thing. Any perceived similarities are just, well, they aren't similar so shut the fuck up about it, okay? This is the Most Fun Place on Earth. Very distinct."

"Cool." Elliott pointed at an obese leprechaun chewing on a white chocolate mailbox.

"This area is supposed to be cleared," he said and then, under his breath as if Elliott couldn't hear quieter words spoken right next to him added: "there can't be any witnesses." Patrick hurried toward the leprechaun. He swatted the portly fantastic creature. "Get out of here!"

The leprechaun growled, spat half-chewed white chocolate mailbox at Patrick, farted audibly, and ran off on pudgy little legs.

Patrick looked down at the miscellaneous debris on his shirt. "I'm going to have to tell someone about that little fucker."

Elliott wandered over to a bench made of cupcakes and sat down cross-legged beside it. He pulled off a cupcake and licked the frosting on the top. "I think I'm dreaming," he told Patrick. "I think you – and that rude little guy – are dreams." He fished out the cigarettes and lighter Patrick gave him. He lit a cigarette and nodded. "It's not a bad dream. Seems long."

Patrick relaxed. Elliott thinking it was a dream was maybe the best-case scenario for both of them. There was a great big Denial Fairy manifesting in his brain. Maybe they were *both* dreaming. He sat down on the cupcake bench next to Elliott.

"You have vanilla and sprinkles on your butt," Elliott advised.

"Not really though," the Denial Fairy said with Patrick's mouth. "Because it's a dream and nothing I do is real."

Elliott took a long thoughtful drag on his cigarette. "Why don't I have shoelaces in this dream?"

"Well, they thought you might hang yourself with them in front of the children." Patrick scooped up some frosting on his finger and licked it. "And that would be pretty upsetting."

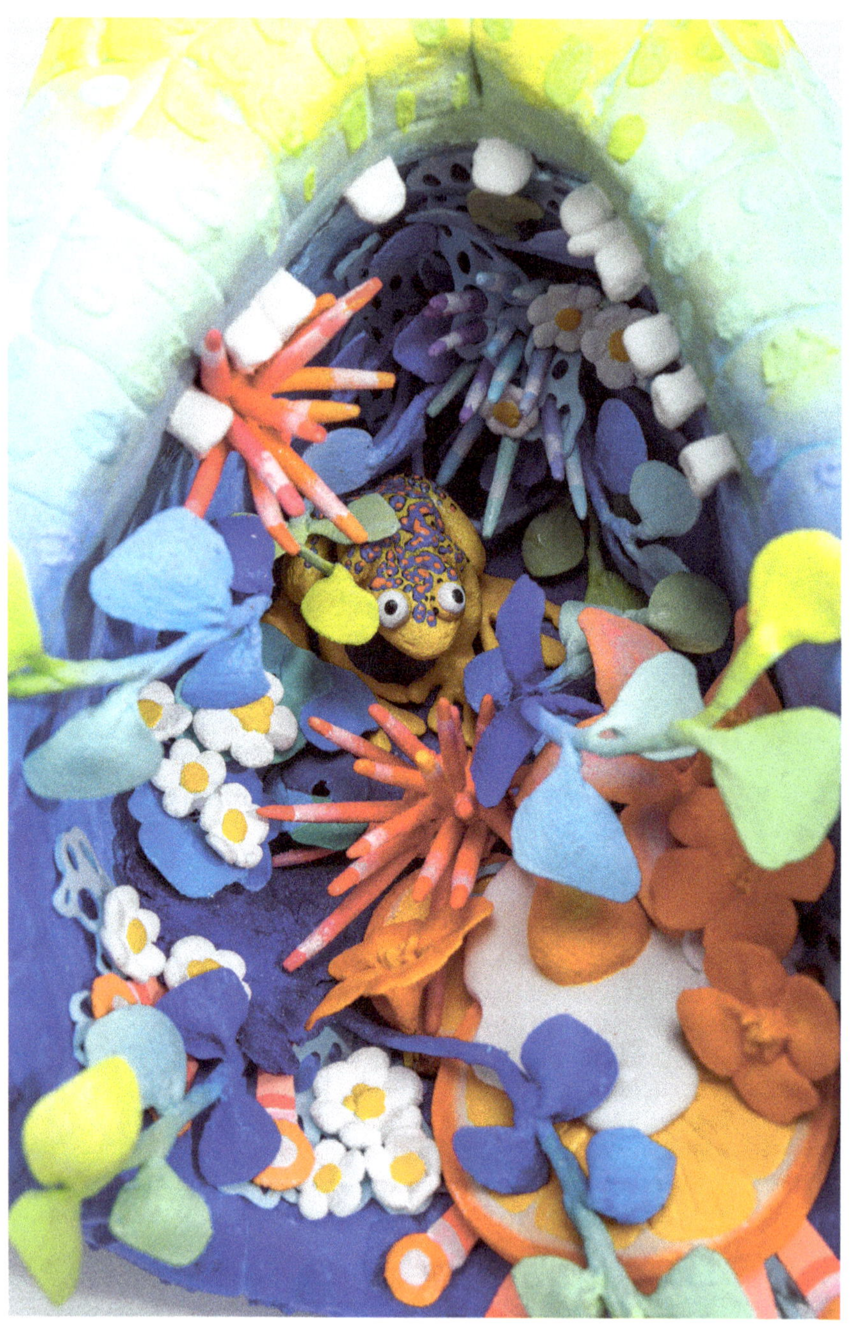

A Frog (with Secrets).

Elliott's eyes widened. "It *would* be."

Patrick looked at the dead singer. "But you wouldn't have, would you?"

"How does somebody even do that?"

"It's a thing in some places. Like certain kinds of prisons. I'm pretty sure it's a thing."

Elliott gestured to a clump of strawberry frosting near Patrick. "Do you mind?"

"By all means."

Elliott dunked his chocolate cupcake in strawberry frosting. "Okay but *why* would I do that?" he asked with his mouth full.

"You're sad. You're a sad, sad man."

Elliott opened his mouth and wagged his cupcaked tongue then swallowed it down, stifling a laugh. "I'm not any sadder than you are," he said. "I'm not sure I'm sadder than anybody at all. I just... I mean, you write a kind of music and that's what people like and that's what you make and it's not like everything about you. It's just a part."

"Like a manifestation. A deep manifestation of some elements of yourself."

Elliott looked off to the side. "Or you have a fan club and a record contract and you do what you're good at and what you're familiar with." He turned to Patrick. "I write upbeat songs with electric guitars too."

"I didn't know that. I don't think I ever heard any."

"That's okay. I don't mind."

Patrick scooped up some of the remaining strawberry frosting. "You're not like I thought you would be and I don't know if that's because you're just a manifestation or a dream or what. I'm not sure you would have ruined a birthday party."

Elliott finished his cigarette and stamped it out on the bottom of his shoe. "I don't think we can both be dreaming."

"You shouldn't really think too much about it."

"Sad isn't as bad as people think it is," Elliott observed. "You can't just eat cupcakes all the time. You'll get a stomachache. And probably diabetes. Sometimes you have to eat vegetables. Sad is like vegetables."

Patrick looked at his frosting-smeared hands. "But cupcakes are better."

"Yeah. I dunno." Elliott shrugged. "Maybe sad can be like carrot cake. Or zucchini bread. But really sad is just... real."

"Real?"

"This dream is nice and everything— I'm not complaining— but if it was like this all the time, I probably *would* hang myself with my shoelaces." He snickered like he didn't know about his Wikipedia page.

Patrick scanned Wonder Town. He had imagined a lot of this neighborhood. The light posts that blew bubbles and the tree that grew toy race cars. Cherry red race cars. Patrick reached into his pocket and put his hand on the gun. "What's wrong with this? It's nice here. People like it."

Elliott scratched behind his ear. "People want things to be all bubbles or all shoelace suicides but... I just don't have that experience with things. This place is just... It's bullshit." Elliott looked over, made eye contact. "It's soulless bullshit."

Patrick started to cry.

"Oh wow," Elliott said. "Do you work here or something?"

"Something." Patrick wiped his eyes. "Sometimes I look at that tree and I think I don't even like cherry red race cars. Someone else has to like them though, right?"

"I kind of like cherry red race cars."

Patrick smiled. "Thank you."

"Are you okay?"

"You ever have to do something that you really don't want to do but you need the severance and insurance?"

Elliott went for another cigarette. "That's pretty specific but in general, yeah." He lit the cigarette. "Carson Daly." He shook his head. "*Carson Daly.*"

"But you did it right? Because you had to?"

"Sometimes I did. Sometimes... fuck it."

Patrick took the gun out. "I'm glad we got to talk today."

Elliott frowned at his cigarette. "How do you wake up from a dream?" He pinched his arm. "Ouch. That didn't work."

"Just close your eyes and wait for the knock."

Elliott jammed the cigarette between his lips. He closed his eyes. "Hmm. Knock?"

"Double-tap."

Patrick shot him in the head. Twice.

Wonder Town was so quiet it almost seemed like there hadn't even been a murder. A puddle of cherry red race car blood formed beneath the cupcake bench. A slow burning cigarette fell from limp fingers to smolder on the hard rock candy asphalt. In the Most Fun Place on Earth even gunpowder smelled like bubble gum.

The white-chocolate eating leprechaun tentatively peered out from behind a light post that was shooting bubbles up into the sky.

"It's okay." Patrick motioned for the leprechaun to come over.

The chubby manifestation waddled noisily with huffs and excess spittle. He hoisted himself up onto the bench next to Patrick and then leaned over and shoved his face into the cupcakes and started to eat.

"This place *is* bullshit," Patrick said.

The leprechaun audibly farted.

Patrick tapped the leprechaun on the back and it sat up at alert. "Do you want to hide in my backpack and come home with me?"

The leprechaun plugged one nostril and blew out some sprinkles. "Do you have a cat litter box?" The creature asked. His voice was a stereotypical caricature of an Irish leprechaun if the Irish leprechaun wheezed and had a lot of phlegm in the back of his throat.

Patrick thought about that question for a long time then turned to the leprechaun. "There's no reason to ask that question that isn't really upsetting," he said. "So I'm going to just ask the Denial Fairy to make me forget you asked it and I'm not taking you with me. I'm getting the fuck out and I'm going to go call my counselor now."

The leprechaun snorted. "Can I have the gun?"

Patrick stood up and brushed off as much frosting from his pants as he could. He thought about Elliott. For the first time he really considered him, considered what he meant, who he was, who he wasn't, who he could have been, and the miscellaneous debris he left behind. He thought about Carson Daly and health insurance, shoelace suicides, cherry red race cars, and Elijah Bennington-Bird's teeth. He imagined a sandwich but his imagination had already been revoked.

"Fuck it." Patrick handed the leprechaun the pistol. He was already fired.

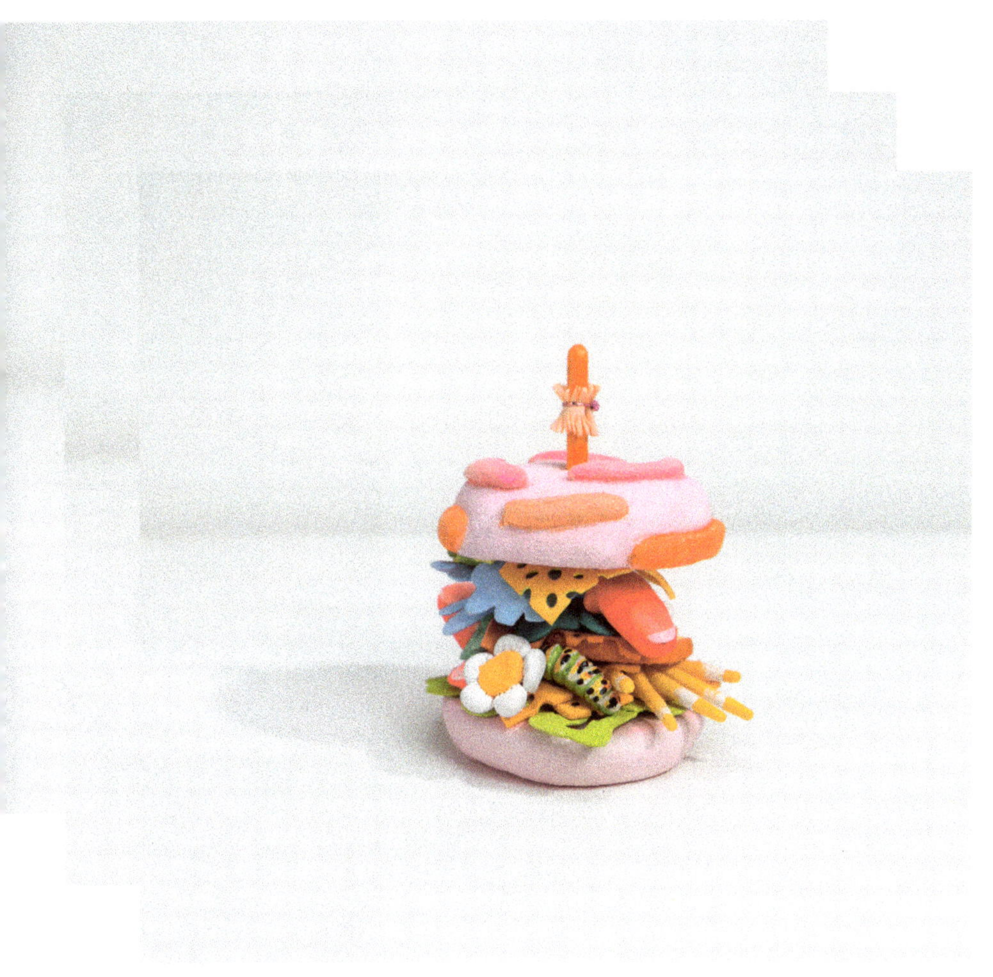

Rosy Slider.

LITTLE DEVILS

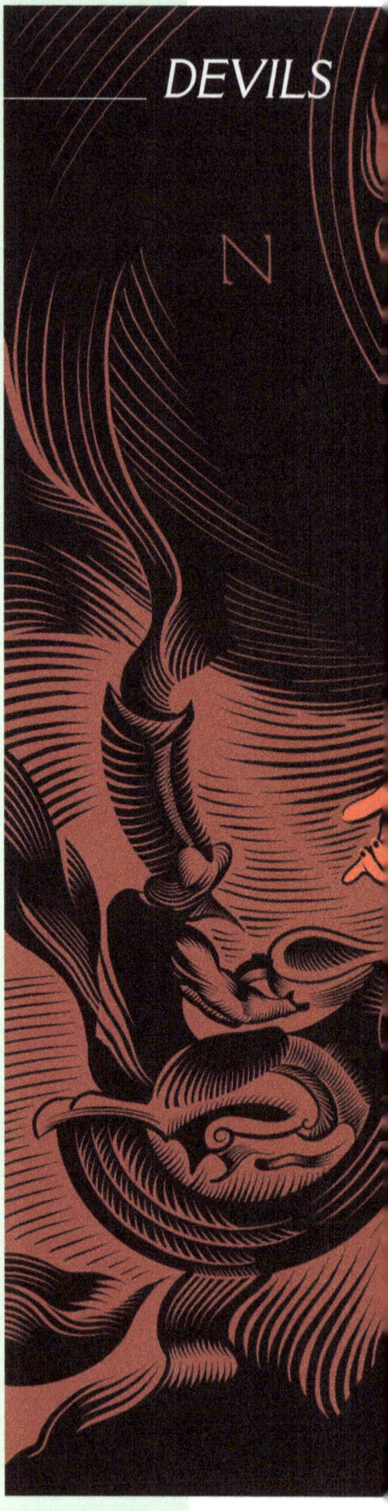

Words: Radha Kai Zan

Art: Tomo77

Radha Kai Zan (they/them) is a writer and artist currently living on the West Coast. They enjoy writing all manner of fiction with a particular leaning towards the weird, the romantic, and the adventurous. You can find more of their work at **www.radhakaizan.com.**

Tomo77 (he/him) is an interdisciplinary artist based in Portland, OR by way of Costa Rica. Driven by the world of circumstance, his work often explores themes of human behavior, capitalism, and pop culture in an immigrant's context. Instagram: **@tomo7701**

12

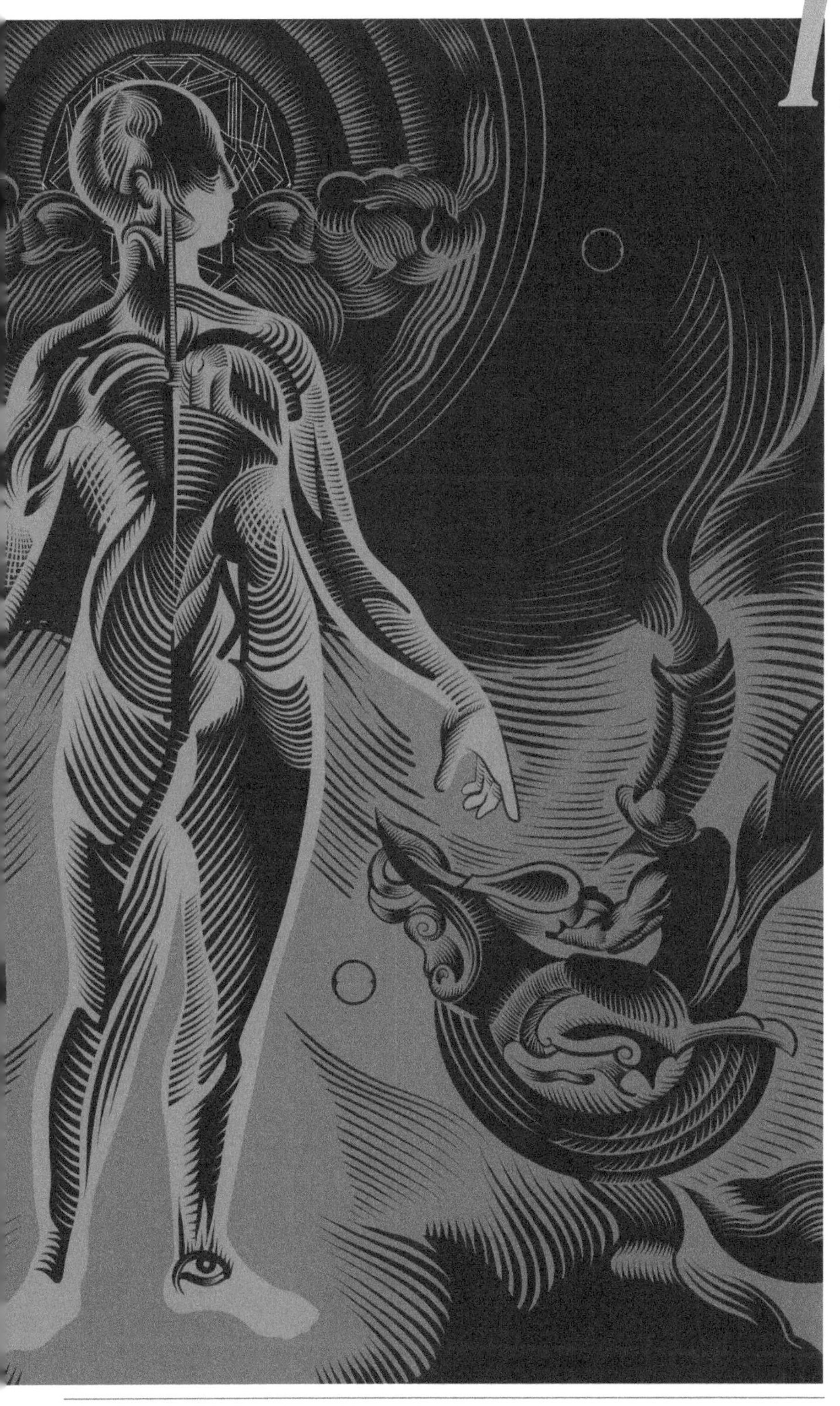

There's nothing more boring than deciding to kill yourself.

I scribbled down a shitty will, gifted my plants anonymously to neighbors and sent my hamster to stay at a petless friend's house under the guise of going on a vacation. I try and imagine the experience my friends or family might have when they come into my house to clean it out, how they'll snoop through my room and my trash. I throw out my dirty laundry instead of washing it, burn a bunch of embarrassing journals in the sink and make sure there's no food that can rot in my fridge. There's nothing worse than opening a fridge filled with putrid milk and old takeout.

When I'm done, I've got two bags of trash on the sidewalk. A whole life lived and the only secrets and shame I've accumulated are in two measly bags. Two tired piles of banality.

"I'm pathetic," I say out loud into the sour afternoon air.

Nothing happens so it's true.

There are fourteen types of lies but I only care about the one I'm telling myself. Fourteen ways to pop out a little devil.

"I've only eaten Vienna sausages for the last two weeks."

No devil; a truth.

"I've only washed my hair once this month."

No devil.

The next words I've been testing out in my head for a few days. Letting the syllables clatter harmlessly against the inner walls of skull. Speaking them separately and out of order, juggling the weight of their meaning behind disconnection. Moving my mouth without the force of my voice.

"I want to die."

And no devil emerges.

***

The neon green weather map is pixel-patched with crunchy piss yellow clouds. It flashes away to the blue of the main backdrop, the pink skin of the lead anchor. The colors lance through my pupils and an instant ache inflates at my temples but I can't bring myself to blink or look away. My body isn't responding to anything my brain is saying like all my nerves have been snipped from their ends.

The last of my artificial motivation is pilled up in an orange bottle in the bathroom, long white capsules bisected with teal. You'd think they'd make them funner, flashier. Maybe then I'd want to take them. Neon pink with purple spots maybe. A little party for your eye. Lively colors because that's what they're supposed to make you want. To live. I think.

Around my feet, my little devils sleep, all sixty-seven of them, spritzed into a temporary coma courtesy of a new Hush! No-Mess Non-Lethal Sleep Spray, Lavender Scented. The lavender smells more astringent like bleachy perfume and I can feel my diaphragm clenching, working up the energy for a punishing dry heave. Their bodies are hot against my ankles, damp and fluttering like soggy fly wings.

I focus on the news instead. Neutral audiovisual stimulus. A digestible pap of sound and color. It's the same regurgitant from yesterday, a lineup of sludgy meaningless headlines:

HIKER FOUND DEAD, POSSIBLY KILLED BY BIG FOOT
NEWBORN PANDA CUB BORN OR COULD BE CHINESE ROBOT SCAM
QUIK-E MART SHOOTING MAYBE DEEP FAKE
BIGGEST PUMPKIN BOAT RACE PERHAPS FUDED BY BIG AG
ANTI-CLONE PROTEST SABOTAGED BY COPS (WHO MIGHT BE CLONES?)

The only devils I see are in the protest footage, clinging onto their sources who are marching down streets and waving signs. Some are no bigger than the pins and patches their sources wear on their jackets. Some wear little doll clothes branded with the current hashtag movement, but others are naked, clinging desperately amidst the churning crowd, falling off to certainly be trampled underfoot.

The current trend is showing off your devils, not to boast the number but to humanize yourself and criticize the demonization of deception in society. I get it, I do, fully support it, but honestly, it's a pretty blatant display of privilege if you're able to feed, clean up after and travel with your devil cadre. I certainly don't have the means to do that.

The segment switches and the anchorman reads off the teleprompter, his eyes black plastic beads, so close together they look more proportionate to a teddy bear than a human. My dad who works janitorial at the news station told me he's married with kids but I can't imagine someone having sex with him, his whiteless dead teddy eyes buttoning down on you over a gaping, gasping mouth trained to say everything and know nothing.

Despite being the ones who deliver the news the anchors are forbidden from researching or watching anything news related. They aren't allowed to keep up to date with current events, as knowing the truth about a subject--or considering it the truth—and subsequently having to lie about it might stimulate the birth of a little devil on air. Before this rule was put into effect, most news was pre-recorded or heavily fact-checked but that was quickly shown to be unsustainable. It requires a bit of mental layering, psychic surrender, and reliable disassociation to never inwardly doubt what you are told to say but, after an intensive 4-month training course funded by an alliance of TV stations, the anchors are thoroughly scrubbed of the certainty of reality. They can say anything with an enthusiastic gleam of chiclet-white teeth and nary a devil will be born. Truth is meaningless in the face of doubt and truth is only trouble.

There was a documentary about the news anchor training program which, while criticized, was generally accepted as a lesser evil. *Lies are how we hold the tapestry of civilization together*, one of the instructors, an ex-military interrogator, had said, *and if we can't lie, we risk unraveling society*.

There was a long interview with him as behind-the-scenes bonus content that had gone viral. During the interview, there is a moment where what looks like a devil is bulging through the top of the man's shirt: a little red pixelated hand grasping through the stitched buttonhole. It cuts away quickly. The clip's popularity came from the debate around what he was lying about. Was he lying about the efficacy of the training program? The pain experienced by the trainees? His own experiences as an army interrogator? That he loved his job?

I replayed it several times, looking for the first sign of devil bulge in his chest or belly—devils often scrambled beneath clothes after they spawned—to pinpoint where the lie had started, but it could have come from anywhere, wandered up from a sleeve or a pant leg. Maybe it was when the interviewer asked about the bite mark on his cheek, a crescent of rectangular indents clotted with foundation but still visible, and he replied with a smile, *Pain is temporary. Quitting lasts forever.*

***

You'd think you would know if you have the will to live or not, like instinctively, but I learned that's not actually true. You can feel like pure shit, look in the mirror and see something half-dead, but when you say it aloud 'I want to die' the devils will let you know if it's true. They'll bust out of you, the exact size and volume of your desire to survive so there's no mistaking it.

That's where my sixty-seven devils came from. The 'I want to die' devils. Just a collection from the last week when I was pissing out the last of my meds, relapsing to my old bloodstream. It hurt to take in light. Speaking was like gagging up stones, each word too big for my throat, every noise popping painfully through the sphincter in my esophagus. Breathing became sucking down air through a pinhole. When I tried to fake a smile to my friends, my mouth tendons moved independently of each other like I was being tased.

So, I started saying it in the mirror or in bed staring at the ceiling: I want to die I want to die I want to die. Sometimes the words ran together into one like a poked yolk—iwantodieiwantodie—but the devils still know what you mean. You can see the gradual change in them, all struggling to make a livable body out of my lie. My almost-lie; a little worm of survival was still swimming in me, but it was easy to smoosh. You can think the life right out of your body, did you know?

Devils one through thirty: the eyes and mouths getting smaller, the joints in the limbs reversing or missing entirely. Thirty-one through fifty-four: some limbs just stop showing up, become torsos pulling themselves around by nubbins that could be limb sprouts or just tumors. Fifty-five through sixty-six: a leech hole in the neck where a head should've sprouted, a squat torso, all vagina. Sixty-seven: a lone arm, inch worming. And then sixty-eight which is nothing.

An evolution of a death wish in miniature.

***

Grabbing food
U want anything

No thx

U didn't eat yet did you
>:(

N ot rnge
*hungry
thx tho

My spiral was obvious to my friend. She'd been good at checking on me, making me open my door so she could ask me face-to-face if I took my pills or if I called in the refill. I tried not to lie because I'm a butterfingers and whenever a devil pops out of me I always drop or fumble them. You never know when they're going to emerge from a more exposed part of your body either, like your face or hands. And I'm not smooth like some people who can brush them away and out of sight as easy as a piece of lint. I have no sleight of hand. I've never seen Shanna pop a devil out when we talked but I refuse to believe it's just because she's honest; she *did* know a few card tricks, after all.

Something itches in the rolls of my waist and I scratch it absently as I scroll through Twitter. I feel something wet burst under my nail and when I bring my hand back, I see two little legs no longer than dime and a string of rusty intestine wedged beneath my nail. Blood seeps into red-gnawed nail folds. Shit. I fish around my fold for the rest of the body and come back with a little glob of meat, splinters of bone thin as hair.

I guess it wasn't that I wasn't hungry, more so that I didn't want to make the effort to eat. Food tasted like Styrofoam and, no matter the texture or consistency, seemed to slide against the back of my teeth in the same nauseating way, a writhing against my enamel. If you've ever eaten a devil, you might know the feeling. Chewy gristle, elastic toothpick bones, the flailing of their little limbs on your tongue, microscopic fingernails snatching at your uvula. It's nasty to admit you might eat a devil but we all do it, like how everyone eats boogers or scabs or sunburned skin sheets. They couldn't run even if they recognized the hungry licking of your lips, the measuring stare.

There's an old saying that goes '*La mentira tiene patas cortas*' because devils will always be around in life. This was a nod to the fact that they would literally be present but also that they physically could not leave the small radius of your body, a distance of three feet at most usually. If they did go beyond the radius and stayed there, which really only happened by force, they would wither and die. I used to be one of those kids at the parks tying up their devils with blades of dead grass and running six feet away just to watch their bodies spasm and choke.

Most parents didn't let their kids keep their devils and not just because of the financial burden of caring for them. It was too easy for children to practice cruelty on their devils out of curiosity. After all, they were still human-like despite their disproportions and apraxia that children found so amusing, they still had blood and bone like us. They experienced pain and sometimes communicated primitively. There had also been a recent study about how kids whose parents didn't curate and monitor their children's devils interactions had a higher chance of engaging in acts of violence against people as adults.

My mom, an esthetician, was thorough about culling all my devils as a kid. She viewed them as not just pests but physical ailments, a type of disembodied acne. It was easy for her to snap them up from where they dropped and pinch their necks in half.

At her work, one of the most popular treatments she offered involved popping ingrown devils from her client's skin, half-formed from a lie left unfinished or too many white lies told. They were mostly harmless but, if left too long in the skin, would often result in deep devil boils which were not just painful for the source but painful for the devils. Because they usually emerged face first, this meant a lot of agonized screaming. They could even die stuck in their pus pockets which looked

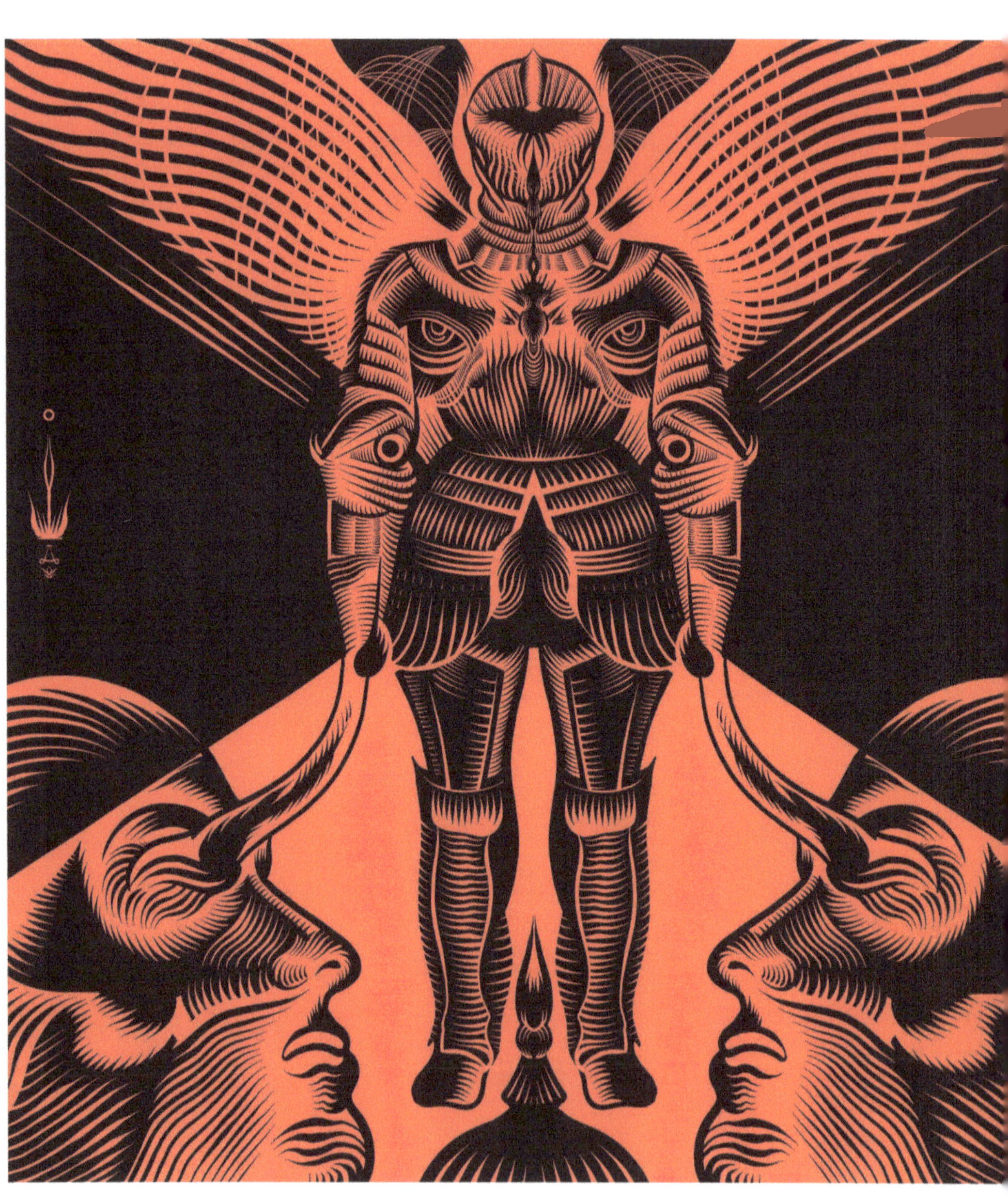

and smelled terrible, like sour meat and rotten eggs.

She never did make much money as an esthetician even though she knew so much about devils. She could list off what they were made of: PGCs, catecholamines, alpha-fetoprotein. More stuff I can't remember but she definitely could. All the money was in psychodermatherapy because even if you could slather someone in retinoids, improve their diet, and keep them from picking their devil-widened pores, they'd never stop getting pock marks if they didn't learn to lie smarter.

***

I start saying my goodbyes which feels trite, egotistical. Writing them out becomes an exercise in convincing myself I'm worth the paper and ink. I imagine my friends getting these letters and simply saying 'Finally' before tossing them in the trash. For my relative, I'm not sure which is the least painful, messages or in-person farewells. I settle on emails to my favorite friends and relatives, scheduled to send in a few days. I don't want to see them in person, hear their opinions on my fat body and ragged skin or to be persuaded otherwise when they clock my mood. I wasn't good at hiding my state of mind or pretending at polite pleasantness. They'd call me out for sure.

I try to think of the last time I saw my parents but it's all a numb blur of depressive amnesia. The first step to suicidal behavior is letting the sadness scrub away your memories, smudge out every happy moment until all that's left is a cumbersome trauma slurry that makes dying feel not just correct but absolutely sane.

I try to recall my abuela and my tutus, but their faces are impressions of impressions in my head, wet napkin pencil renderings. My abuela is the most prominent in my memory, mostly because I dislike her. She always made a show of calling out my devils, snatching them up and shoving them in my face before spanking me or saving them in the fridge for later to show my mom how much of a little liar I was. *You're not my granddaughter, you're just your mama's mentito aren't you?*

In Latin American countries, they'd taken to calling the devils mentitos. Little lies. In Hawaii, they called them punis, a word that meant deception but also to 'gain control of' or 'overwhelm'. They weren't cute, mostly, not like the Anglo epithet *little devil* made them out to be and which denoted some canny impishness. No, they tumored off from your body and wriggled into existence with the same level of detail your lies contained: a precocious lie might give you a complete mini simulacrum of yourself, usually the span of your hand in size, pin-boned but whole, maybe with the features bulging unnaturally or the proportions just slightly off. These it was appropriate to hide and dispatch of in private, as they were a product of advanced subterfuge and more or less insulting in a social setting. The more traumatic the lie or larger the magnitude of truth the lie obscured, the smarter the devils got. Some spoke, parroting a mantra of your worst thought loops back at you. Some, spawned with extra lungs, could scream for hours at a time without losing any volume.

An off-handed 'I'm good' when you weren't, might bear forth a single leg, three inches tall with an eye, sometimes not even a mouth to speak or eat or breathe. Those didn't last long, often gasping and seizing without the means to process breath or nutrients. It wasn't unkind or uncommon for a source to simply pluck the devil up and shove them into their pocket and mercy-smother them, smear them quickly under the sole of their shoe.

It was impolite to point these kinds of devils out. Everyone slipped up once in a while and you didn't want to hear the truth anyway, right? And who even knows what truth is, anyway? Humans think they're so smart but what do they really know? It's healthy to be skeptical. Besides, the antidote to devils is doubt. You want to stay in the safe gray space between the binaries of black and whites.

"Question everything" an old white motherfucker once said. There might have been more to that quote but that's the only part anyone remembers. Question. Everything.

And so, we do.

***

I swear I tried. I made the effort. I did the med trials, the therapy, some ECT. I tried exercising–runner's high. Endorphins? Never met her–but that seemed to make it worse. When I lost weight my skin ended up sagging, the bags under my eyes drooped, no longer puffed out with fat. Less of my clothes fit and I couldn't buy more so everything hung off me like a caul.

"You look so much healthier!" my friends would say. "So skinny!"

But they never said I looked good or better because it wasn't true.

"Babe, you're isolating yourself! Of course, you're going to feel bad," they'd chide me. "You need to get laid A-S-A-P. Have some fun!"

I didn't have the heart to tell them isolation was just a symptom. Nothing outside could help; it was in me. It was innate. But I tried. I tried because one night when my friend came over to check on me, takeout in hand, her mouth tightened, and her eyes got sort of hollow as she looked at me. The face of someone who realizes they just stepped in dog shit while they were out trying to take a nice walk.

So, I let her sign me up for Cinder and I eventually matched with some guy with a crooked nose and eyes that naturally made his face look it was smiling even when his mouth wasn't. We tried to have sex but I couldn't get wet as expected and the cold lube made my stomach twist when he tried to push inside me. I told him it was my fault that I couldn't get wet, not him, and he looked genuinely understanding and then like I'd just laid down a challenge. *A dry pussy is one of the saddest things in the world*, he said.

He didn't sound disappointed but I knew he was. Who wouldn't be? I felt so pathetic and dead, a desert embodied. It was such an easy thing I needed to do, too. Be a hole. I couldn't even be a hole for someone. That's how alien I was now. I wasn't even made of the same material as the rest of humanity. I was calcified. A broken bone.

He tried eating me out, but I had to push him off. It felt like a truffle pig sniffing around in soil. He tried dirty talk and ending up telling me visible labia were cool. It was trendy not to like them, I guess. *Girls today always look tucked in. Like when you push Kleenex back in the box.*

I gave him a hand job for his troubles even though my tennis elbow was acting up. As I jerked him off, I noticed a bunch of scabbed pits around his shoulders, his upper back. Devil exit wounds. Had he been lying during our texts? Had he been lying while he was dirty talking and squirreled the devils away before I noticed? Then I realized he hadn't ever actually complimented me IRL, just compared and contrasted the state of my pussy neutrally. I felt irritated and then latched onto that irritation like a buoy, thrilled by the sudden sensation.

Suckling on the irritation, I got it in my head to try something I'd read on some Seddit back in the day. A mean little experiment. As he got close I asked him to tell me I was beautiful. He did instantly, face shriveled shut, brain clearly off. Of course, he couldn't mean that. I was sallow, drooping and my skin was coarse. I felt like a mangy dog, the first sign of rabidity stirring in my skin.

And then I felt it. Something sharp and rigid in his dick like a fishbone working its way up to the head and then he screamed, high like a smoke alarm, and shoved me away. Rolling on the ground, I could see a half-formed devil arm poking out of his dick, flailing, struggling to emerge.

I had to help him work it free with tweezers because its tiny foot ended up lodged in his urethra. When I finally extracted it, he pushed me from his apartment, sniffing back tears and cursing under his breath. He smashed the little cum devil onto my chest. *By the way, I lied! Your pussy look like an Arby's roast beef sandwich, you crazy bitch*!

I jumped back before the slamming door could bust my nose open. The squished devil smear sat like a red petal on my shirt. Its dime-sized hand lay severed on the toe of my shoe, its only fingers left the thumb and the pinky. The smallest shaka in the world.

***

Like most lies, the devils ended up being sketches of their source, small fleshy caricatures, a cartoonist's cruel impression of your inner self. We called ourselves sources and not parents because they were not children even with the familiar dopey innocence they often had or petulant vehemence they conveyed through spitting tantrums and barking gibberish. It was an insult to compare them to children, really. Animals too. They had more in common with pox than people. Doomsdayers said they were divine curses we needed to nurture as penance. UFO cults believed it was an extraterrestrial pathogen leaked from Area 51. But both groups usually kept to the internet.

Animal rights activists and anti-abortionists were the noisiest, descending on the issue of the ethics around devil dispatch like vultures on a fresh carcass. Their zeal and rhetoric around the right to life quickly adapted to the little devils conundrum. Just because they weren't considered intelligent didn't meant they should be exterminated the same as one might cockroaches or mice or traditionally sized, traditionally born humans. Their status as a pest to the majority of the population did not give their source the right to kill them. In fact, you had knowingly created the tiny being, so it stood to reason that the responsibility fell to you for its continued upkeep and contentment.

There are other ugly arguments the pro-devil movement has made (they prefer the term facets over devils) but that is the one that sticks with me the most. I used to spend most of the day convincing myself that I wanted to be alive and then I have the gall to force these little facets out of me to experience the same shitty life? Hungry, angry, sad, in sick and malformed bodies. None have ever seemed suicidal like me though, even with all the apparent reasons to.

They were actually voracious little things. I mostly couldn't afford to feed mine the popular kibble it was trendy to give them. I let them lick my food wrappers or take-out containers clean which seems like enough for maybe ten of fifteen of them. When I forget to feed them, they scrounge finger and toenail crescents off the floor, chewing them like white watermelon rinds. They don't mind eating hair clots or skin flakes from the baseboards either.

This might sound like everything is cleaner when they're around but they still shit and piss and vomit, though I usually kill the ones that do it uncontrollably. Most of mine are potty-trained and go on a newspaper by the trashcan; they learn fast when you rub their nose a few times in their messes. It's weird pushing your own tiny face into a little dollop of shit but you get used to it.

***

The second phase of emancipating life from body: impressing on yourself that nothing matters, especially you. When truth doesn't matter, neither does reality or self, the abstract or actual. It creates a nice causal chain. Nothing means nothing is nothing. And nothing feels worse or is more freeing than knowing whatever you do will have no effect on anything else.

So it stands to reason I might as well be dead, right? I don't know why everyone hasn't come to this same conclusion. Why they aren't belting their necks or gargling pills. That I might as well be dead is the sanest thing I've ever thought. The distance between feeling dead and the idea of being actually dead begins to close the more I meditate on it. It's the only thought working itself free in the gray matter fugue of my brain, a little botfly of a notion being born.

What sucks is that even if nothing matters, the world still keeps touching me. Like it can't stop digging its thumbs into my eye sockets, trying to pop them like broken yolks every time I have a vision of how my life could go. And what can you do but stand there and take it, seized by the rigor mortis grip of chance and existence, a never-ending enervation.

I tried to see if my devils ever got tired because they each do one thing. They do this one thing, pass out, wake up, eat, and do it more. One of them, all body no face, loves to stomp around in circles like a little Henry Hawk. Another, a leg with some torso and half a head, loves to thrash up and down, jackknifing in place. Some sleep constantly as if depressed but I can't tell if they're sad because they still eat with gusto. Some make certain noises, chattering punctuated with deep manly screams. There's one that's just an arm and the mouth is where the shoulder socket is; it can't move much so I keep it by my phone to remember to bring it along.

Some people say they have personalities but I don't think that's true. Like, you get one trait and suddenly you're an archetype? A fully fledged individual? A random mutation of cells doesn't make a person. Even a person doesn't make a person.

***

Memory, reality, truth, all of it gone or glazed into obfuscation. If you can't trust the government or culture or gods or men, then you can at least trust yourself, right? Wrong wrong wrong.

The body is the easiest lie to tell. The third step towards permanent existential absence: disassociation from flesh. This will either be the shortest step or the longest. For me, it was the longest.

My skin began to grow necrotic, feeding off dreams of grand self-annihilation but really, I was just rotting away from routine and rote rituals of survival. Working to maintain a dead life, to house a dead body, to keep the body clean of flies. Flavor sloughed off my tongue and pain roosted in whatever crevice of cartilage it could find. Muscles began to tense without my control, atrophy when it should hold. My tits and stomach fill out rapidly from the cheap shit I manage to scrape into myself and then they unbloat into loose satchels of flesh. Color bleeds out of my eyes and soon each blink lasts an hour. Sounds diffuses to static and my voice loses all volume. I get hives and fevers for no reason. All my shits turn watery and yellow no matter what I try and eat.

This is the last gap my mind must close, the slit between the feeling dead and the being dead. The body acknowledging the limits of existence and the benefits of not. You can make a conspiracy of your own death, rant about it until your brain whispers it to the rest of your meat.

"You're better off dead."

No devil. The slit winks shut.

***

I'm a good swimmer so it can't be drowning. I have a delicate stomach and am prone to projectile vomiting so pills and poisons are out. I'm afraid to spew acid back out. I'm not great with knots. But falling seems simple enough. Hard to stop the process of gravity once you've committed.

I have nicer clothes but I don't want to make a scene. My nice clothes can be resold too, go into a little rainy-day fund for my parents. I settle on loose jeans, yellowed tank, big ol' flannel and scummy Timbs. When I leave my flat, my devils are already sprinting to catch up, toppling down the stoop, snagging the hem of my jeans for a ride. The slow ones die behind me, drop into little wet kernels of flesh. The sidewalks are shiny and red with lies.

The bridge isn't far and I can feel the circuit finally closing in my head—dying, dead, dying, dead, dying, dead—and it's like my skin is coming loose, parachuting off in perfect silken billows in the wind. The follicles of my hair feel pumped full of helium. My tongue is a smooth cool stone in my mouth, my heart a perfect fist of dry ice. Every passing sound smoothes through me like a Percocet.

I walk faster downtown, up the on-ramp shoulder to the highest point of the overpass. I think about jumping in front of the car but if my aim is off or they swerve I might just end up paralyzed. There's only about twenty devils left, all of them hanging onto my pant legs, gasping for breath, trembling. I scrape them off with my boot heel and then climb over the barrier. Below is a crisscross of freeway underpasses. It's early enough for traffic to be light. Beneath that is train tracks and track ballast. It's an ugly spot to die, a crusty tapestry of gray on gray, but its high and besides, gray seems right. The flavor of my life.

The devils make their way to my side of the barrier through a drainage hole and start to cling onto me again. I decide the easier thing to do is stomp them all to death, so I do. The drop, as fast as it will be, would kill them slower than my boot would. When they're reduced to a sad puddle of offal, I shake my limbs out and toe up to the edge like I'm going to shoot a free throw.

Head down, I think. Need to try my best to swan dive, make sure my skull connects first. I heard it's faster that way and, if the impact doesn't kill you, the bone shrapnel from the rest of your skeleton transiting through the rest of your brain is insurance. A swan dive is insurance. A swan dive is a swan song.

***

They used to think the devils were some sickly spiritual manifestations. There's all sorts of old self-help books about how to tap into your inner truth, to digest shame and transcend deceptions. But if the devils were sent from god as some means of a moral teaching, would it be so easy to get rid of them? To feed them to your dogs or local wildlife. Put them down the garbage disposal. Spray them with Devil Off! which worked within seconds. And what was the intended lesson? Pity for lesser creatures? We already had those. Empathy with these little disturbed facets of us? Didn't god know how good we were at disassociation?

I always think: if god wanted us to be hampered by our lies, he should've made our devils bigger. Giant deformations of us rupturing free through some splashy sarcoid osmosis, running around, screaming and thrashing. Real brimstone inferno nightmare shit. That would've really driven the point home.

That's why I know there's no god. Because you can live an entire life without a single lie bothering you. Because you can kill a devil for $1.99 plus tax.

***

I jump.

***

Once I gave a devil a steak knife to see if they wanted to hurt or kill the other devils or me or itself. It was a patchy-colored devil with all the right limbs, a suggestion of an oblong head on no neck. It had a penchant for biting.

I made it hold the knife, pinched its hands between my thumb and index, and puppeted it to cut another one, just so it'd know it could. No reaction. I made it cut itself, just shallowly. It shivered and made a little 'ah' sound. It held the knife for a second before dropping it, falling back into their usual routine movements.

That's why I know they're not worth saving: they're too stupid to know when they have grace in their hands.

***

Headfirst, eyes watering, wind, cold wind, black hole stomach, hot piss squirt, and fast fast fast swallowing air. The second before the full brunt of gravity and asphalt unites to pulp my head and rocket skull shards into my brain, my life flashes before my eyes: graygraygray and a million mediocre memories per second flicker through my mind's eye, colorless and empty, and then I'm coming apart like confetti, little devils bursting all at once from my pores, screaming dog-whistle high as they jigsaw free, hundreds maybe a thousand pulsing out, splitting off in one great and meaty fission.

I'm not lying, I think as my forehead starts to cave and all my devils shrapnel out into the world in one wet red firework.

I want to die, I think as my ribs being to flatten against the ground, my bones collapsing easy as papier-mâché.

I don't want to live, I think, and my tongue makes a devil of itself in my mouth.

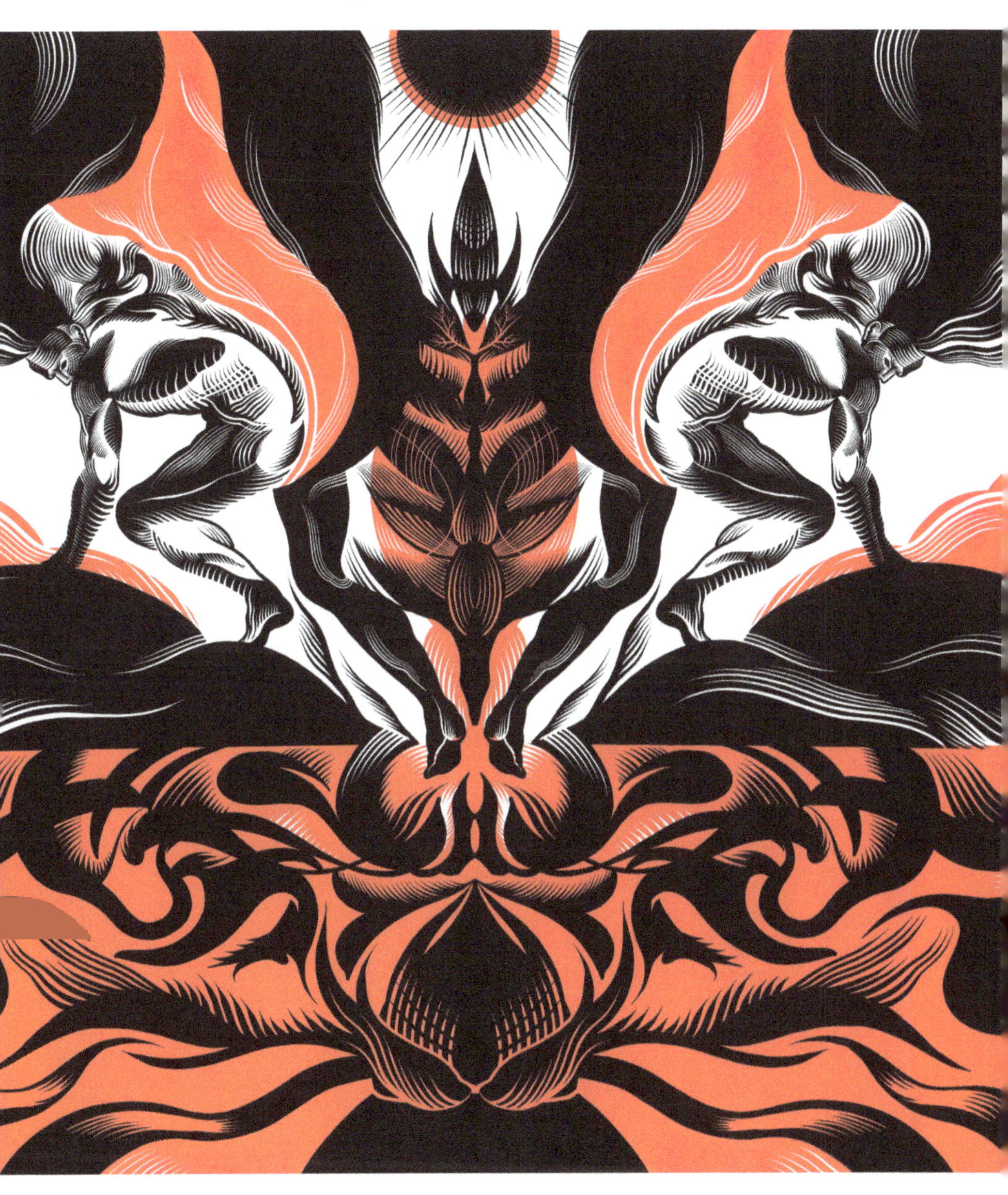

HOW THE OFFICE WINDBAG UNWITTINGLY HANDED ME THE KEY TO KNOWLEDGE

Words: Andrea Coghlan

Art: HELLSEA

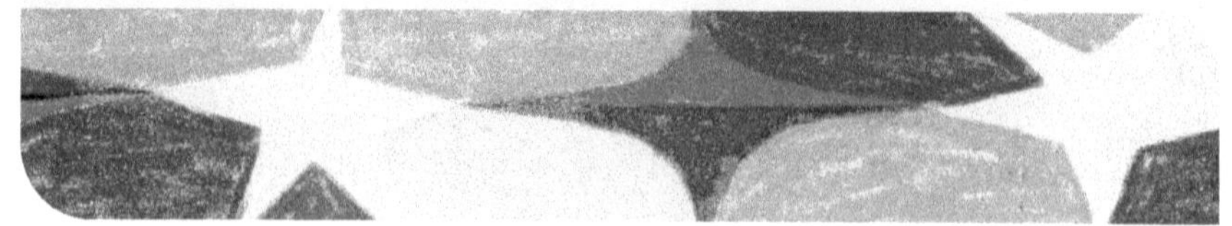

Andrea Coghlan (she/her) is an Afro-Panamanian writer based in Portland, Oregon. Her work has appeared in *The Seattle Times, Scary Mommy,* and *Atta Girl Magazine*. She is represented by Steve Troha and Jamie Chambliss at Folio Literary Management and is finishing up a book proposal about her Black (and White) ancestors who held slaves in Jamaica during the Georgian period.

HELLSEA is the creative vision of Chelsea Wilkinson (she/her), an Asian American multidisciplinary artist in Portland, OR. Her work centers around romantic existentialism: expressing the love within the reality of simply living, and how to create in art the moments and sentiments she finds about life that are intimate, joyous, and magical.

Instagram: **@iamhellsea**

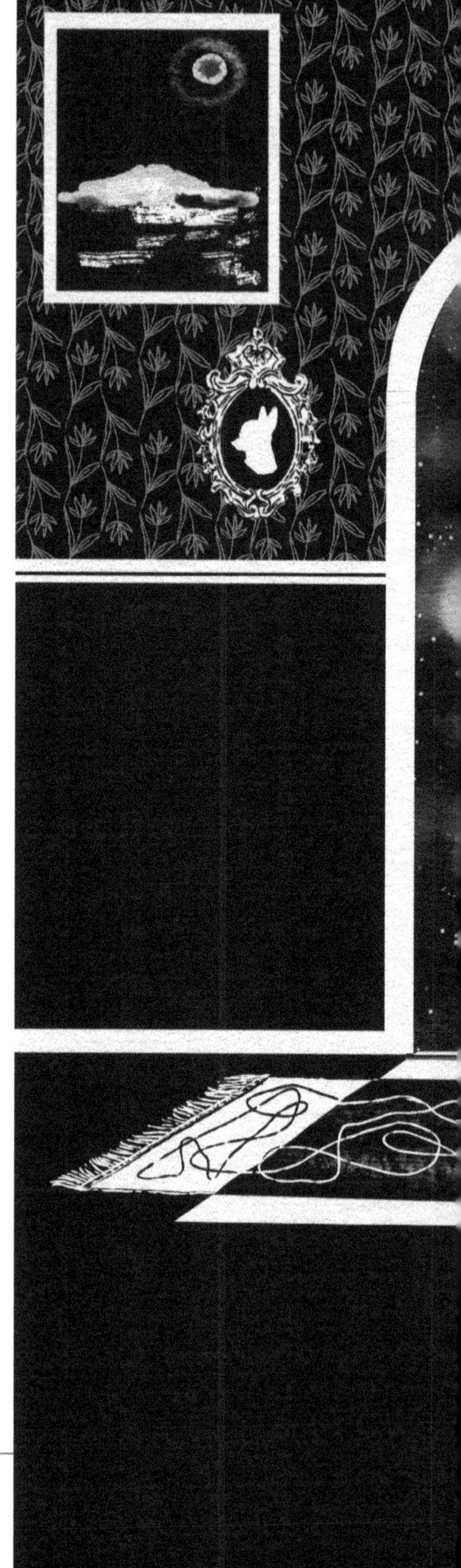

It's not cute to admit this, but I've been feeling myself lately... intellectually.

In the past few months, I've read a *Brief History of Time* and *Astrophysics for People in a Hurry*. I've been sniffing around theoretical, astro, and particle physics as well as cosmology. I've been considering the possibility of multiverses and trying to conceptualize the edges of black holes. I've been getting down to brass tacks adult crap, too, like dabbling in the stock market. Not speculation or anything like that but buckling down and learning how to make compound interest work in *my* favor for once.

I don't know you, though.

Maybe you have a glittering career in finance or are an actual scientist. Maybe you don't find my reading list or my "accomplishments" particularly noteworthy. That's cool.

But maybe you *are* like me.

Maybe you've taken a remedial math class or two in your time. Maybe you'd rather tweeze your pubic hair strand by strand than attempt to mentally calculate a 15% tip. Maybe you can't remember any string of numbers longer than

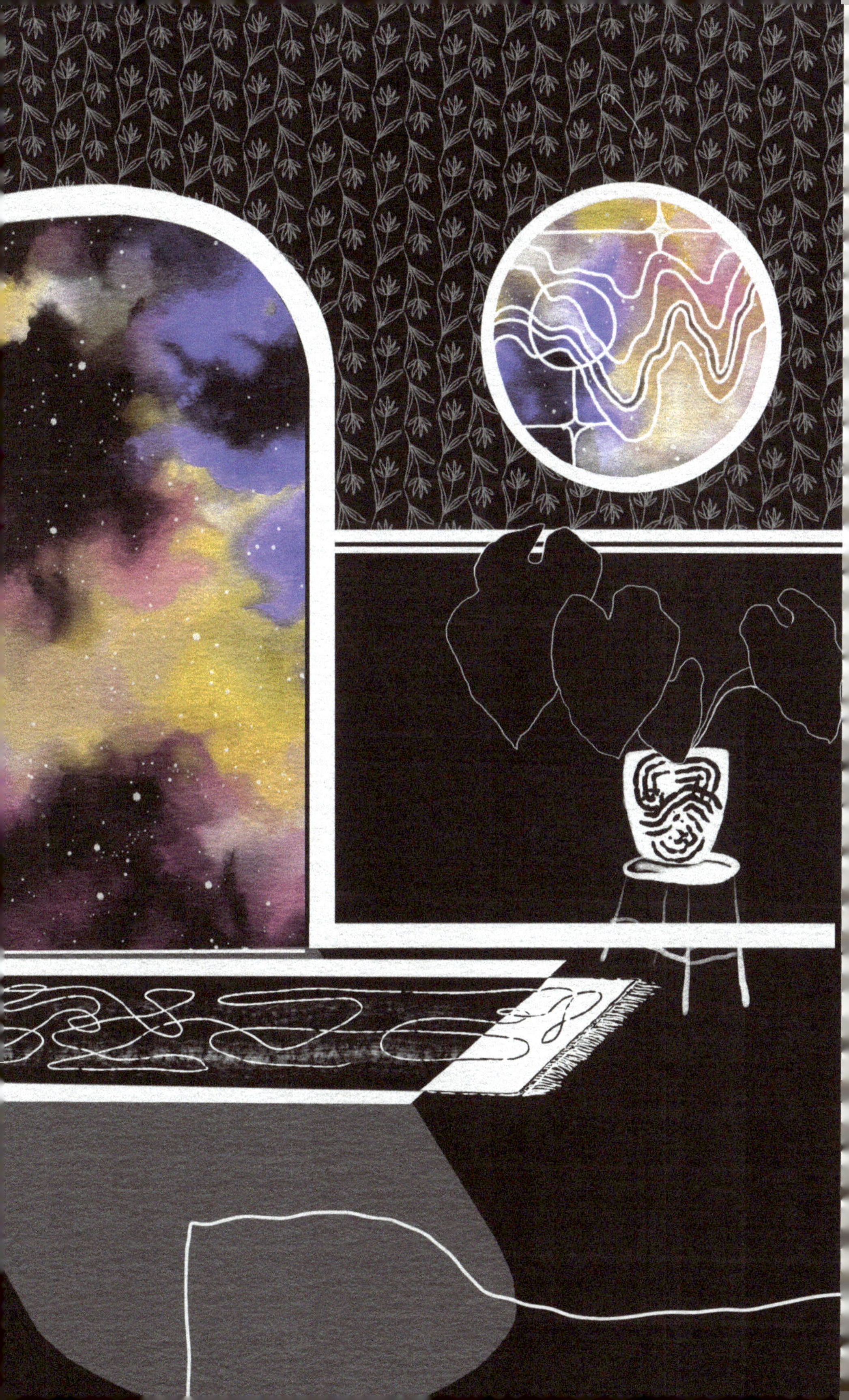

four digits. Maybe you're more familiar with the cast of all *The Real Housewives* franchises than the components of an atom.

Maybe you believe you are better off sticking to subjects you naturally excel at, like the arts and the humanities. Maybe you think numbers and equations are best left to your more left-brained compatriots.

I know that's what I believed for a very long time.

In school, it quickly became apparent that math was always and would always be too hard for me. Any attempt I made to prove otherwise killed my little spirit. And since math was a problem for me, it came as no surprise when learning about science was also a no-go. I understood my rightful place: in Ms. Kelly's fourth-period art class, drawing blind contour portraits.

Fully convinced that STEM was none of my business, I vowed to (over?) compensate for my deficits with my natural creative flair. This approach worked reasonably well for nearly two decades— garnering me a degree and jobs with progressively better titles and bigger paychecks.

And it was at the last job — among the noise-absorbing, taupe-tinged cubicle walls — that I had an epiphany.

On a nondescript workday I found myself in conversation with a colleague. The colleague in question was considered an expert on everything equity, diversity, and inclusion by many in our organization. And so, it made perfect sense that equity, diversity, and inclusion would be the topic at hand. Honestly, I don't remember much about the specifics of the conversation, except that it felt less like an exchange and more like him fire hosing me into submission with a relentless stream of jargon. Between his use of phrases like "building capacity," "holding tension," and "taking learnings to scale," I felt my focus drifting to the tangerine and emerald-colored diamonds adorning his fuzzy pullover.

Then it suddenly occurred to me. There he was — this Black man — trying to explain to me — a Black woman — the intricacies of racism and other forms of oppression in the workplace. And for a moment, he tricked me into believing that what he was saying was over my head.

Like I had not spent my entire life navigating the world as a Black person with a vagina. Like it had not been at our same workplace where someone assumed I was a summer intern five years into my tenure. Where I was confused (on numerous occasions) with Rashida, another Black woman who worked on the other side of the building. Where a coworker asked me during an elevator ride why I'd gone for such a "radical" hairstyle after cutting off my tidy, office-friendly locs.

Why was this so-called equity and inclusion aficionado speaking to me so opaquely? What was he trying to hide? Was it that he wasn't in the mood to have that conversation? Was it that he didn't know what he was talking about? Or was he weaponizing technical language to box me out of the "conversation" and assert his sense of superiority?

It made me wonder: what other bits of knowledge had been characterized as being beyond my grasp by people and institutions with authority over me? What areas of expertise might I have mastered if they'd simply been presented to me differently? Would I have had more drive to trudge through the skills that vexed me if someone had clued me in on the "real world" value of their mastery?

Look, I don't want to come off too whiney about this. The things that I excel at have gotten me far in life. Far enough to where I have the luxury to stop and consider how I might improve my situation by re-examining the learning challenges that I once believed to be insurmountable.

My natural interests in story and identity have attracted me to the work of those who have validated my experiences in this world—voices like Ta-Nehisi Coates, LaToya Ruby Frazier, and Nikole Hannah-Jones. Thinkers whose work helped me connect the dots between the stench of injustice perpetually singeing my nose hairs and malevolent systems working tirelessly to uplift some by standing on the backs of others. (See: redlining, school segregation, disinvestment, etc.)

It made me wonder: how could I apply this new insight about systems into my life? Which systems duped me?

I'll answer the second question first. The American educational system duped me.

Not a single teacher helped me accurately identify my math-based learning disability, and as a result, I was never given the appropriate support or accommodation. Not to mention the practical application of math in real-world situations being obscured at every level of my schooling. Don't get me wrong, I by no means think I'm special. I'm among the scores of American students who have and will continue to be robbed of financial literacy instruction. Call me a cynic, but it's almost like someone, somewhere, has a vested interest in keeping future consumers ill-informed about their money for as long as possible.

Which brings me back to that first question: How do I apply the insight I've learned about those malevolent systems to my life?

These days, whenever I feel that a person or an entity is attempting to paint a concept as being beyond my grasp, I notice. I ask myself if that person or that entity has anything to gain from my ignorance. I won't assume that said person or entity is acting in good faith, nor do I accept that just because I don't understand something instantly that I never will.

When it comes to the subject of math, I've made peace with the reality that I'll always probably have to work harder to grasp concepts that might come easily to others. That's fine. I have confidence in my ability to find the answers to the questions that may arise. I have the skills to identify reputable teachers.

Don't believe me? I've paid off my college loan, car loan, and credit card debt in under a year, thanks to what I learned from a book entitled — I-shit-you-not — *Rich Bitch*. And now, instead of paying out of the ass in interest to fend off my bloodthirsty creditors, I'm leveraging interest to grow my investments and cultivate more generational wealth for my family.

But enough about money.

Something unexpected and far more profound happened to me once I faced my fear of math.

Suddenly, learning about science was back on the table too. Why the hell not? And by golly, satiating this newfound curiosity is helping me cope with the mounting social, political, ecological, and economic horrors plaguing our world.

I find the looming existential threats facing our existence far more palatable when I consider the age and expanse of our known universe. I'm tickled that

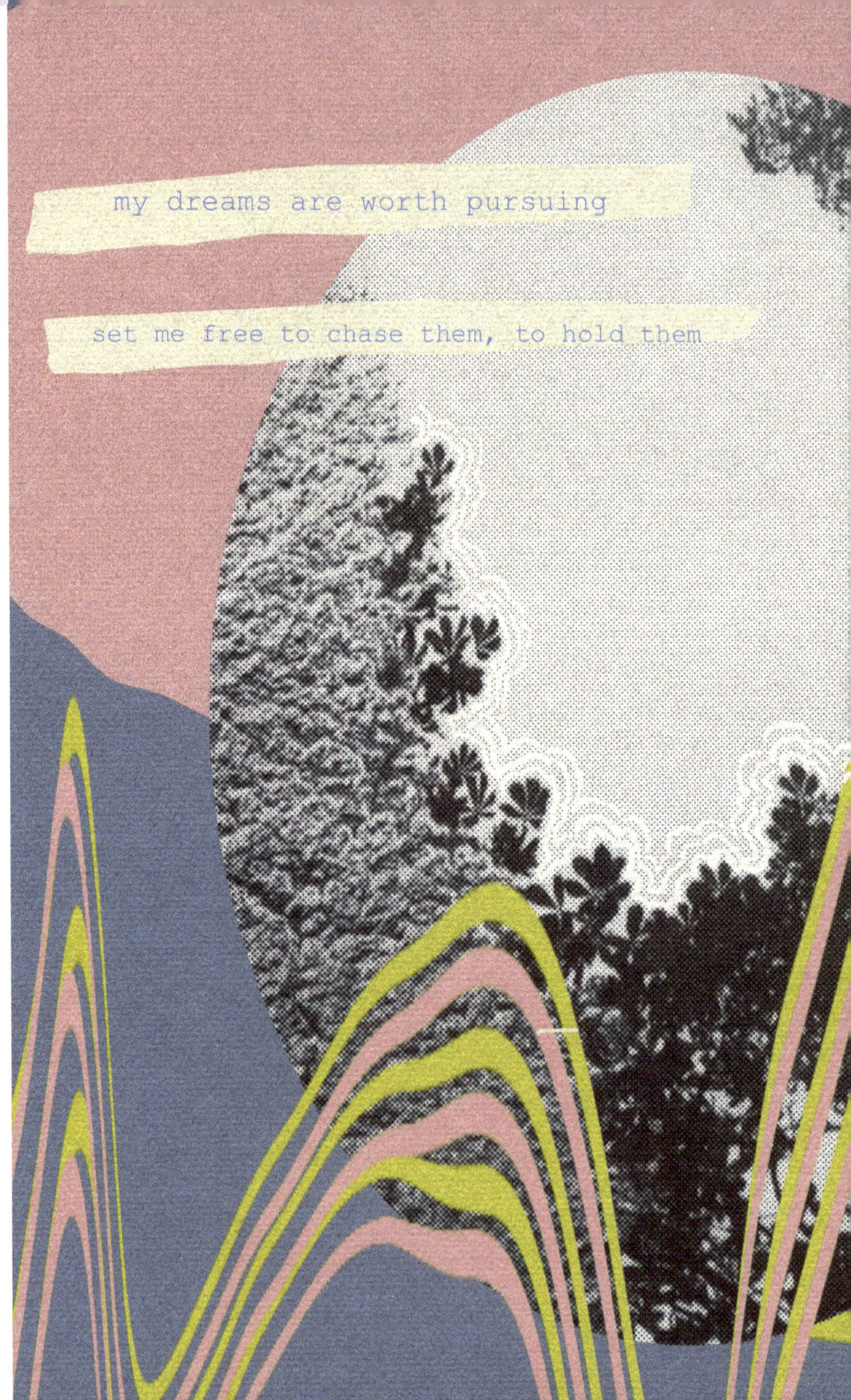
my dreams are worth pursuing
set me free to chase them, to hold them

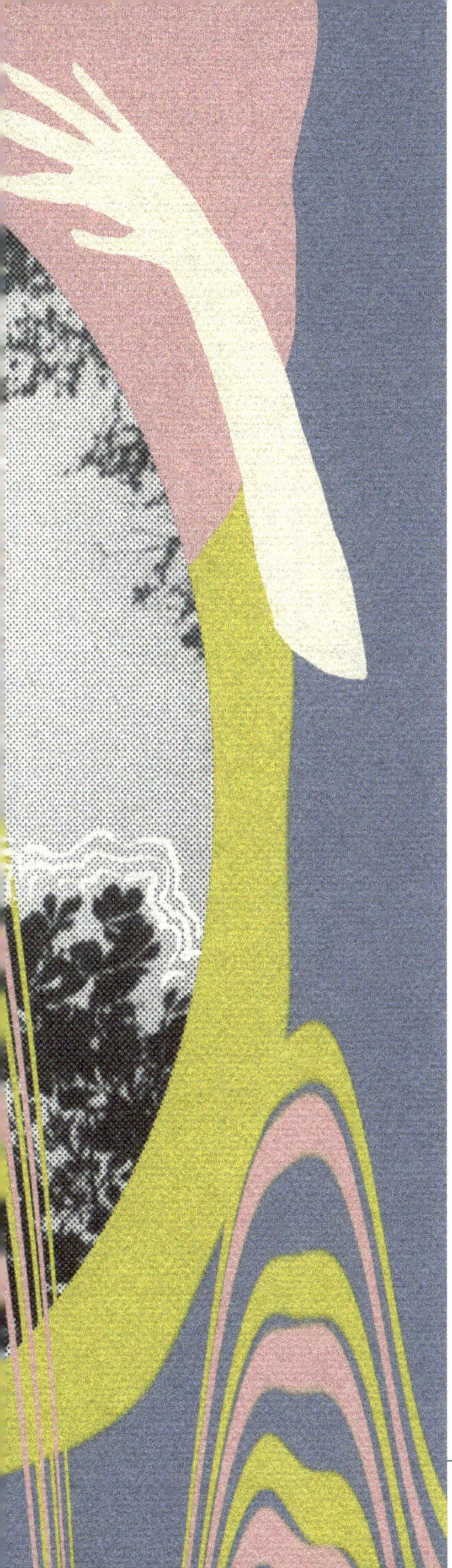

those things I was told as a child were fiction are actually literal lines of inquiry being pursued by some in the scientific community, like the possibility of multiverses and even intelligent life beyond our planet. And I'm not sure why, but it honestly brings me hope that somewhere else in this universe (or another), existence isn't quite this...fraught.

On a brighter note, I'm so grateful that scientists like Carl Sagan, Neil DeGrasse Tyson, and Emily Levesque have dumbed down their lives' work to make science accessible to the layperson.

Of course, there's so much I don't understand about science or a great many other topics. But now, instead of that feeling like a moral failing, it feels more like an invitation to learn. Because if there's one thing that I've internalized from my new foray into science, it's this:

No matter the subject, I'd rather chase my curiosity than surrender to the notion of incomprehensibility.

TUMEFACTION

Words: Matt Kolbet Art: Emily Elizabeth Wise

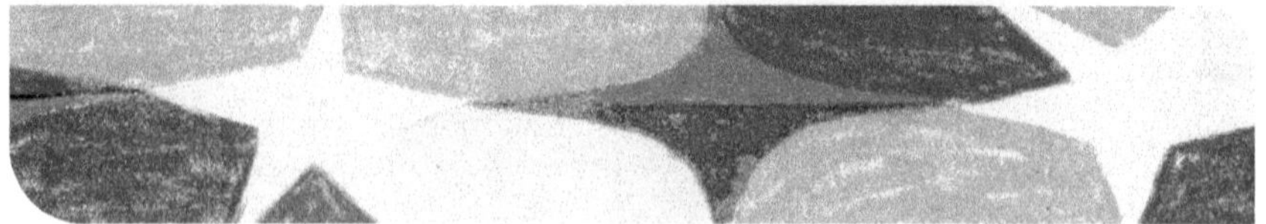

<u>Matt Kolbet</u> (he/his) teaches and writes in Oregon.

<u>Emily Elizabeth Wise</u> (she/her) paints landscapes and still lifes. Except that's not true, because they are actually feelings and experiences disguised as plants, mountains, skies, structures, objects, and weather. Using paint as an echolocation device, her work explores the surreal meeting of inner and outer worlds that leave you feeling both lost and found. She stays hyped on big feels, the S-shaped line that separates yin and yang, Elaine de Koonin's still lifes, rain sounds, female surrealist, and a certain shade of purple she has dreamt about but can't match.

Instagram: **@emily_elizabth_wise**

One of the passengers was complaining, but she wasn't wrong. The bus was hot. Not just hot, but downright sweltering, and although it was only May, as summer rolled in the heat would intensify. The bus shared the essence of all travel in Florida: desperation.

Everyone bloats.

Otto had driven the route from Tampa to Englewood for more than fifteen years. It was one of the better routes, known among the drivers, who often ranked and re-ranked routes over beers at the end of a shift, as a sweet deal.

Otto's route avoided most of the tourist traps, and because of its length, usually meant idle passengers who merely wanted to get from their point A to some point B and the promise of better times. They were ones to believe Marcus Aurelius' *Meditations*.

All wishful thinking. When it got so hot, there were never better times. Even water was temporary relief at best. Doesn't help that you're fat either, thought Otto, but he exaggerated the smile on his face and blinked at the woman.

"I am sorry, ma'am. The mechanics will have a look when I get back to the depot tonight."

The mechanics would do no such thing. If possible, they were lazier than the drivers, jealous of a job where you could sit most of the day. They resented dirt on their uniforms, rushed work, and the way managers condescended to them, never seeming to avoid that singular phrase: "Just get it done."

The woman accepted Otto's attempt at ingratiation and sat down, grumbling to herself. It didn't hurt that Otto was a large man, too. Though short of giant status, and its corollary, gentleness, his form retained some of the vigor of his youth, someone who might have been a colossus.

He knew his trade.

If a bus was late or hot, the supervisors offered apologies, but it had to show up. People needed to get to Tampa and Venice and, god help us, even Bradenton.

Otto lived in Bradenton, which meant driving up to Tampa to pick up his bus each morning, before heading south and then back again and again, an automated yo-yo of repressed spite.

They had almost reached Ruskin on the journey north when the gears of the bus seemed to catch and grind. Otto managed to pull the mechanical behemoth to the side of the road before a thunderous clank settled the issue of where they'd stop.

As he pocketed his keys and pulled a lever to open the door, the woman who'd groused about the heat stood up.

"Be cooler outside," she said, not wanting to share the vehicle's apparent spiritual confusion. She might have been right about that, too, and since Otto didn't know what was wrong with the bus, or how long it would take to fix, he let her go.

"Don't go roaming," he said. The shoulder sloped to a shallow, dirty puddle, almost the size of the bus. It looked unnatural and Otto only had a moment to wonder how it hadn't evaporated already. Traffic roared sporadically on the

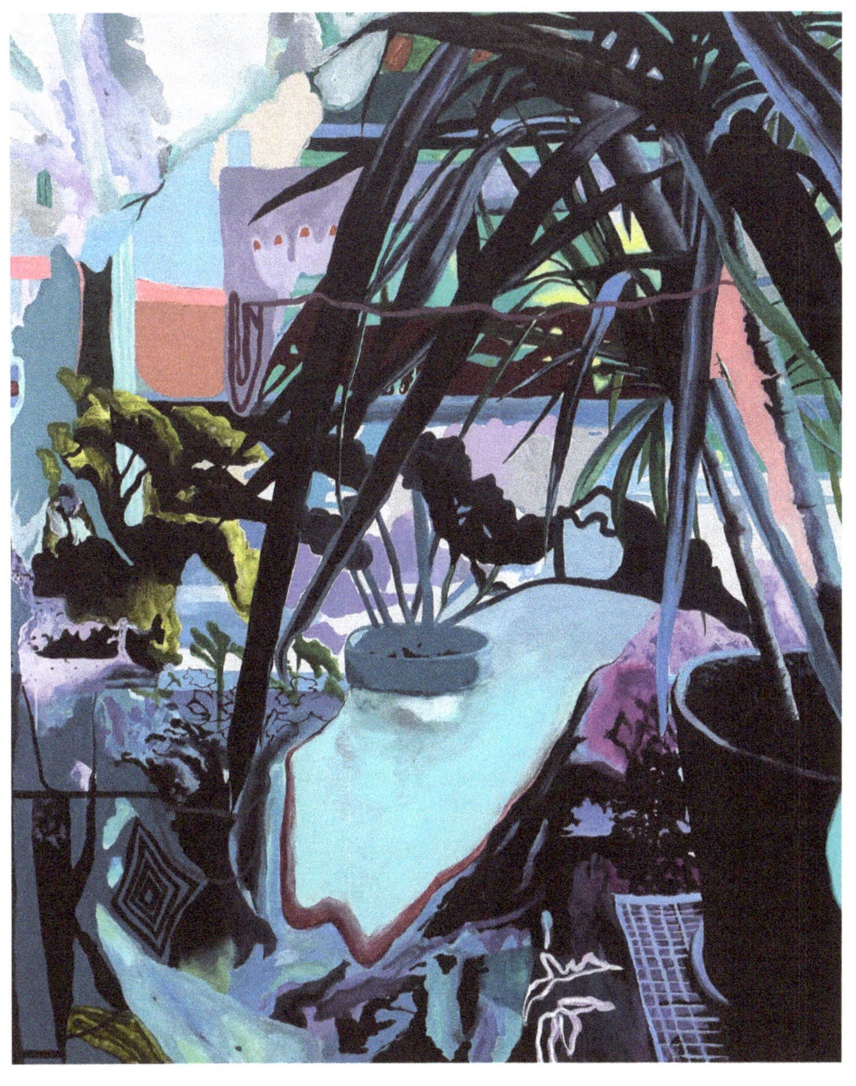

Flood My Machine.

other side of the bus. On these freeways, it wouldn't take much for a rushing car to careen into the bus or some hapless soul on the side of the road. Only the bus would be able to take the blow better. And as the pavement warmed, tires would stretch to breaking. Even light hitting the windshield might blind a driver and that would be it.

Sometimes the whole world seemed to lean on light. Planets begged stars for it. It led wise men. Fools, too. Still, in the dark everyone fell to fooling faster.

He watched the woman pace back and forth and scoffed.

He glanced at the engine compartment and said a prayer. Through the windshield he saw that the woman was the only one to leave the bus. Everyone else possessed secret information. OR they were content to sit, cooled by patience. They knew a stoic's view on coursers in the circus.

"Try the battery box," Otto muttered to himself. If something was wrong there, probably be easier to fix.

The vehicle's metal frame was still hot, so he licked his fingers and undid the latch. Sure enough, a wire had detached. Funny. That had never happened before, not in all his years driving. And it had never come up when the other drivers talked over their routes and passengers and far-away dreams.

"First time for everything, I guess." He fixed the displaced wire and closed the box, happy traffic had been light. Unthreatening. The cars that had passed seemed wary of a sidelined bus. Crossing to the open door, he spied the woman walking, waltzing almost, murine on her feet, more scheming than the recipient of some unknowable breeze.

"Be a minute," called Otto.

He heaved himself up the stairs. Sat. When he turned the key, the bus started without coughing and the seated passengers cheered.

"Gonna risk it," he said, shutting the engine off once more. He wanted the quiet so he wouldn't have to move again, and leaning, he called out for the woman. She didn't answer. Cursing silently, Otto hoisted his bulk up once more and plodded down the stairs.

It felt brighter outside, like the blinding clarity after a storm.

The woman had moved away from the bus. She was staring into the vast puddle, as if it mysteriously cooled the air around her. When Otto opened his mouth to call her again, a long, lethal creature thrust itself from the water. Its movements were swifter than the eye, which mainly tracked how the water splashed as prodigious jaws opened to bite the woman's leg, flashing a row of terrible prehistoric teeth.

Impossible havoc. The water in the puddle couldn't be more than a few inches deep. But Otto could see the beast dragging the woman behind it, like a kidnapping husband in old tales.

She must have screamed, for her mouth was open, but a big rig blasted past the idle bus, loud enough to drown out any protest, and large enough to make the bus shudder.

Otto looked over his shoulders. The other passengers were tracking the truck, cowed into disbelief by its speed and size. When Otto had made up his mind to rescue the woman, there was no sign of her. Another impossibility. Even a famished alligator couldn't take down a human in so short a time, let alone digest her. Perhaps there was a congregation of the animals, usually pushed back from the road, but driven to fraught acts by hunger.

Except the gator hadn't seemed hungry, only eager.

Though there was no sign of the woman, the alligator—Otto was certain it was the same one—returned to the edge of the shrinking puddle. That was something, too. The puddle was vanishing quickly. The final straw was how the animal caught Otto's eye and winked.

"She wandered away," Otto found himself saying. He was on the bus again, unsure how he'd mounted the steps or closed the door or found his seat. "Probably only going as far as Ruskin and got tired of waiting."

What he was thinking was a different matter, a line of poetry by Walcott: *things must fall, and so it always was.*

No one objected to his lame and truncated explanation. A few people glanced out their windows, but there was nothing except a shoulder that drifted over a swath of baked mud, grass, and eventually swamps. A complicit silence lasted the rest of the way to Tampa.

After Otto dropped off the bus, one of the other drivers invited him for a drink. Shaken, he turned the man down, saying he was too tired. When he pulled his car into the driveway almost an hour later, Mary seemed surprised to see him.

"Everyone else busy?" she joked. Otto shook his head and she read his face. "Everything okay?"

He didn't know what to say. The heat she would understand. It wasn't the first time a bus had broken down on his long route. But the woman and the alligator were beyond words.

"No, just a long day."

"Well, you got some mail." She handed him a plain white envelope and he opened it with a calloused finger. Inside was a letter with a heraldic seal. The Thalia Jacaré Society. A raffle he'd won.

"It's money," said Otto. Mary looked up and he handed her the letter. "A check, anyway."

"Says you've won their raffle." Mary scoffed. "Probably a scam. You put it in your account and suddenly a hundred bucks goes missing. Enough people fall for it and it's a revenue stream."

Mary's bookkeeper brain was always suspicious.

"Online maybe," said Otto. His fingers tightened on the check, wrinkling it. He didn't remember entering any raffle, but what of that? Age made him liable to forget. Maybe it had taken a long time to process. Maybe fate saw good news was overdue. "But this is a physical check. That wouldn't work. The bank would verify it first. They'd have to."

"Still seems a bit dodgy. And we don't need the money." Mary's face brightened. She hugged Otto suddenly, kissing the top of his head. "Or maybe this is a charity gesture. There's a winner, but everyone knows they're supposed to give at least half the money back." Otto nodded absently.

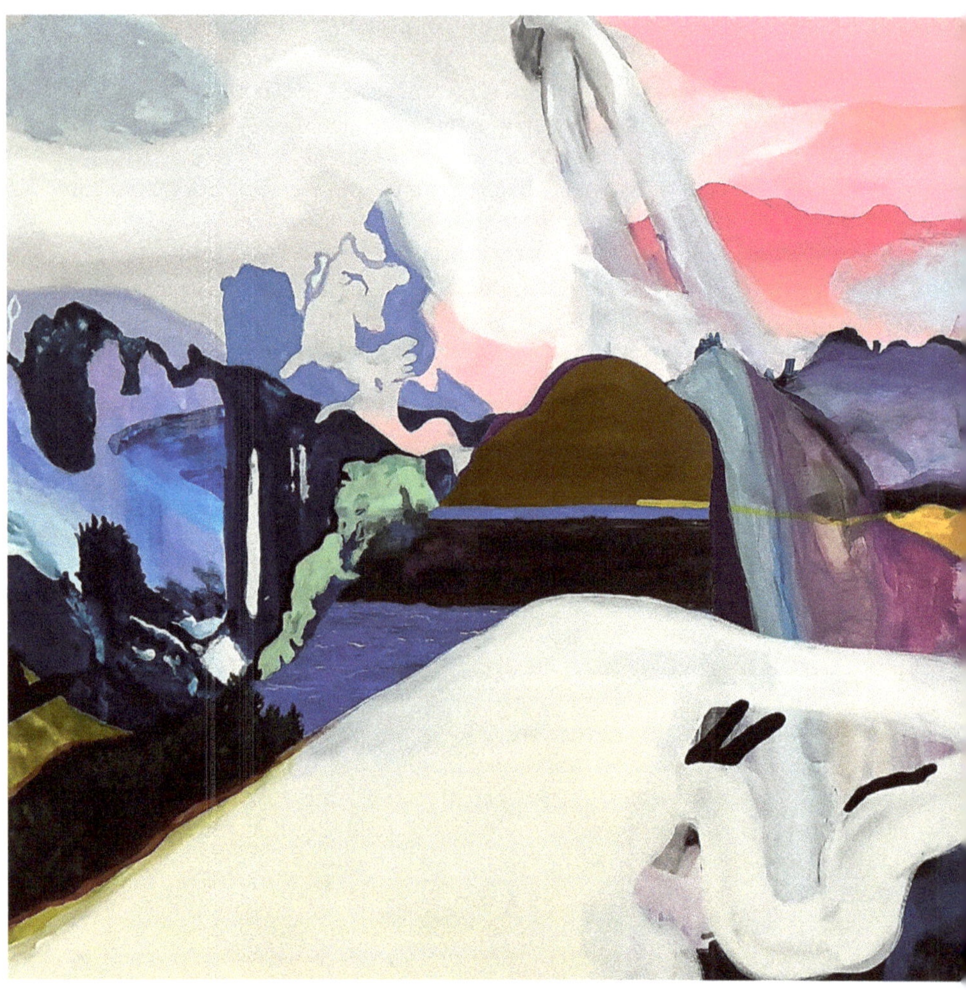

Over the years Mary had seen hundreds of creative ways to raise money for churches and libraries and shelters. "Maybe this Jacaré place is wildlife preservation or something."

Otto nodded wordlessly again. The letter hadn't said anything about the group's mission, only that he'd won.

Such fortune made him feel like a kid again, after his parents' divorce, getting twice as much at holidays to compensate for the fracture. He'd learned to expect it. After his father's unexpected death, the gifts and trips, no longer a product of competition, dried up. Life showed its brutal edge. Closed doors. Apologies. Vague encouragement to keep trying. By the time he graduated high school, he was spending more time on the streets than indoors.

Before he met Mary, falling in love with her and her beliefs about the world's virtue, he'd learned how to steal from sidewalk cafés, trained himself in timing. When to pause. Where to look. How to run without seeming criminal.

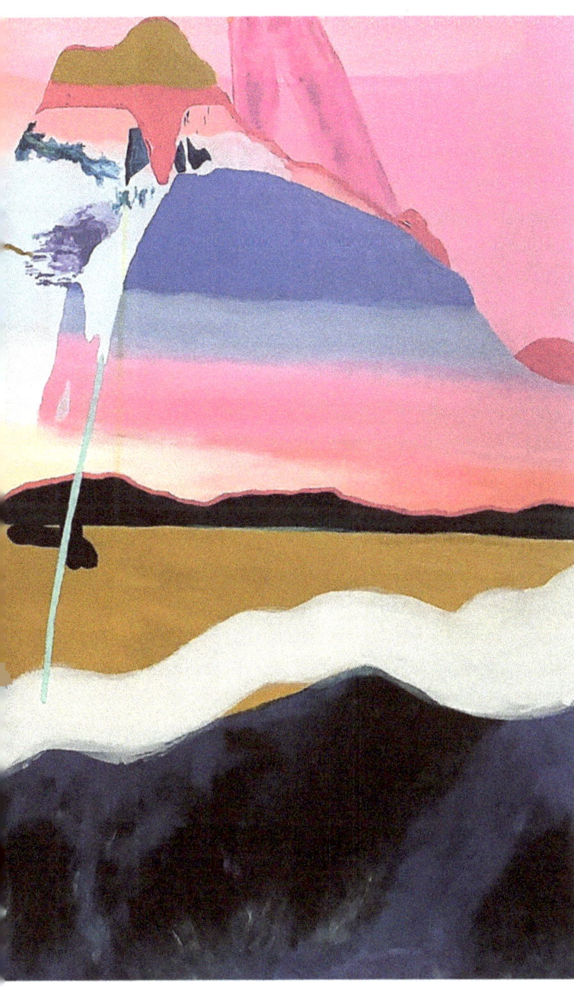

Yes.

And the rolls he'd stolen, the pastries and uneaten meats that helped sustain him, had tasted better because they were illicit. He'd absorb the intoxicating odor before satiating his never-ending hunger.

He lifted the check. Impossibly, it emitted the same enchanting scent.

He was busy counting the zeroes. He forgot about the bus's troubles, the woman disappearing, or the alligator winking.

***

Otto wasn't exactly complaining a few days later when the weather cooled briefly. He put it as a hypothetical in the darkening depot.

"Let's say you've won some money. And I mean a lot. Tens of thousands, maybe."

"How did I win it?"

Otto laughed. "That's what it comes down to it, isn't it?" He'd been too busy imagining roaring into shops, no more quarreling over what bread they could afford. He'd buy what he damn well wanted. Walk drunk on the pavement and not care.

"Let's just say a kind of lottery."

"Then I'd enjoy it."

Otto had wanted to. But Mary had made him look up more about the Jacaré Society. Online information was thin, barely a shadow, though he discovered that Mary had been correct. Past winners, one of the few things listed on the website, were quoted as saying how surprised they were to discover they'd won, and how good it felt to give back. The whole thing was circular, and seemed like a scam, a ride that could go on forever. The website thanked its thousands of donors, anonymous of course. Only prize winners were named, at least those who had decided to share their unexpected wealth with the same organization that had favored them.

Mary had said he didn't have to give it all back.

"A percentage would do. Then you'd still have enough for us to take a nice trip, or put a down payment on a car. And everyone would see your name, your generosity, online."

Otto had said she was right. But he didn't want a new car. He was sick of driving.

"Enjoy it," Otto repeated to the other driver, thanking him as he strolled toward his bus. The morning drive was always the longest part of his day, a trip with no horizon.

After exchanging passengers at Englewood, he made up his mind.

Buses, after all, were just mobile caskets. Everyone, including Otto, headed the same way, to songs of slaughter. The world had no time for idylls anymore. If epics existed, they were tales of long-suffering families or criminal decades. Twisted facts. Otto didn't desire anything grand, only something more than the claustrophobia of these days, moving from the driver's seat to the depot toilet.

As he approached Ruskin, Otto looked for the mirage of water, that vast unaccountable puddle. When he spied it, he felt a jolt of happiness. He'd known it would be there.

He grunted loudly, hoping he sounded surprised, and edged the bus onto the shoulder.

"Just the heat," he said to put his charges at ease. It wasn't a particularly hot day, though shutting off the bus would mean the air conditioner would stop running. "I'll need to look at the engine. Cool it down some." His heart was a hummingbird. "If you need to stretch your legs or catch a breath of fresh air, feel free."

No one appeared inclined to accept his offer. A few passengers shoved down the sticky windows and a fainting breeze coursed through the waiting bus.

Otto looked at an elderly man near the front, a chap who probably had family in Tampa, sons and daughters who loved him, just not enough to make the long drive to pick him up. People who figured the bus would suit.

"Sir, fancy a chance to move about a bit? Still an hour to Tampa."

The old man grunted, hardly encouraged, but got off just the same. He was the type of man who would sing when asked, though he was liable to count the measures, anticipating the end. After tottering off the bottom step, he didn't seem to know what to do with himself.

Otto watched over his shoulder. Coolness was not this man's concern. Curiosity might be.

"How do you suppose such a puddle forms in this heat?" The old guy took a step. He was a hound for knowledge. Probably hated nothing more than an empty hand or empty words.

While Otto made a show of grumbling near the front of the bus, his passenger leaned over the water. He dipped the toe of one shoe into the water, though it didn't take mouse-trap motion for anything to happen.

It was just like before.

An alligator, the same one he was certain, caught the man's leg, dragging the body away in an instant. Soon there wasn't even the memory of a splash. And as with the first time, the puddle contracted rather than dissipating. Soon the only thing on the side of the road would be flat land that transformed slowly into swamps.

Otto didn't wait for the alligator to wink. The gesture made him uncomfortable, complicit in a deadly game.

"Nothing to do when folk just wander off," he complained as he sat and mechanically closed the door.

A woman near the back of the bus protested.

"I've ridden with that man before. He's got family he visits. What are they going to say? Better call the police."

Otto shrugged, but he pretended to make the call and pretended to pray afterward, looking up through the ceiling. Whatever god was listening had blessed him a second time.

The old man's daughters and sons would assume he'd missed the bus. They'd telephone first, and contact the bus company, tracking down schedules and credit cards, maybe even resort to bulletins and online petitions, but it would be like counting holes in the universe.

When the day closed, no one asked Otto to join them. The reptilian look in his eye warned them away. His breath was foul enough without beer. He raced home to Bradenton, happy to drive only himself, to sing loudly off tune. Money wouldn't cure his every pain, bring back withered flowers, restore the beauty of past lovers. But it could keep a bowl full, a glass brimming.

There was nothing in the mailbox, and he assumed Mary had collected it already. He'd sift through the pressing bills for a white envelope, another installment of unearned joy.

But the counter was empty. The house quiet. The evening hot. Sometimes you wanted to scream, as if that would make a difference.

Sighing, Otto took off his shoes and trudged to the bedroom. He called Mary's name and got no reply. There, on his pillow, was the note she'd left—he'd almost expected something like this. Delight could take its thousand forms and might seem poisonous gas or a warrior or an aging vase. It didn't have to be virtue, and this was not. This was hardscrabble love.

Mary, the note informed him, was sorry. Was going away for a while. The money bothered her, and she hoped Otto would give it away. If not back to the Jacaré Society, then to someone else. Their needs were met. She'd put away some savings, a little secret. They could take a trip, something to remember.

So it went, on and on.

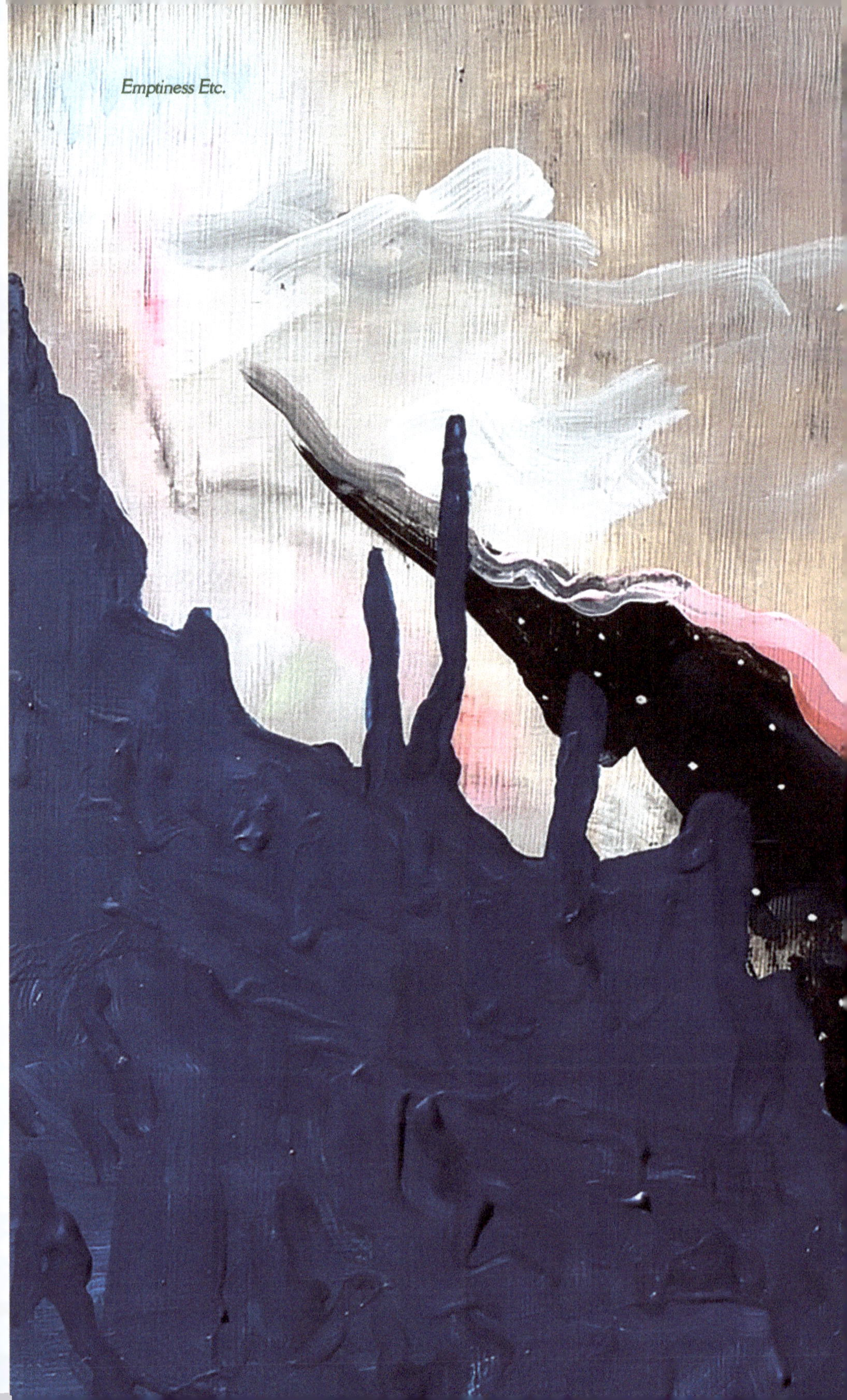

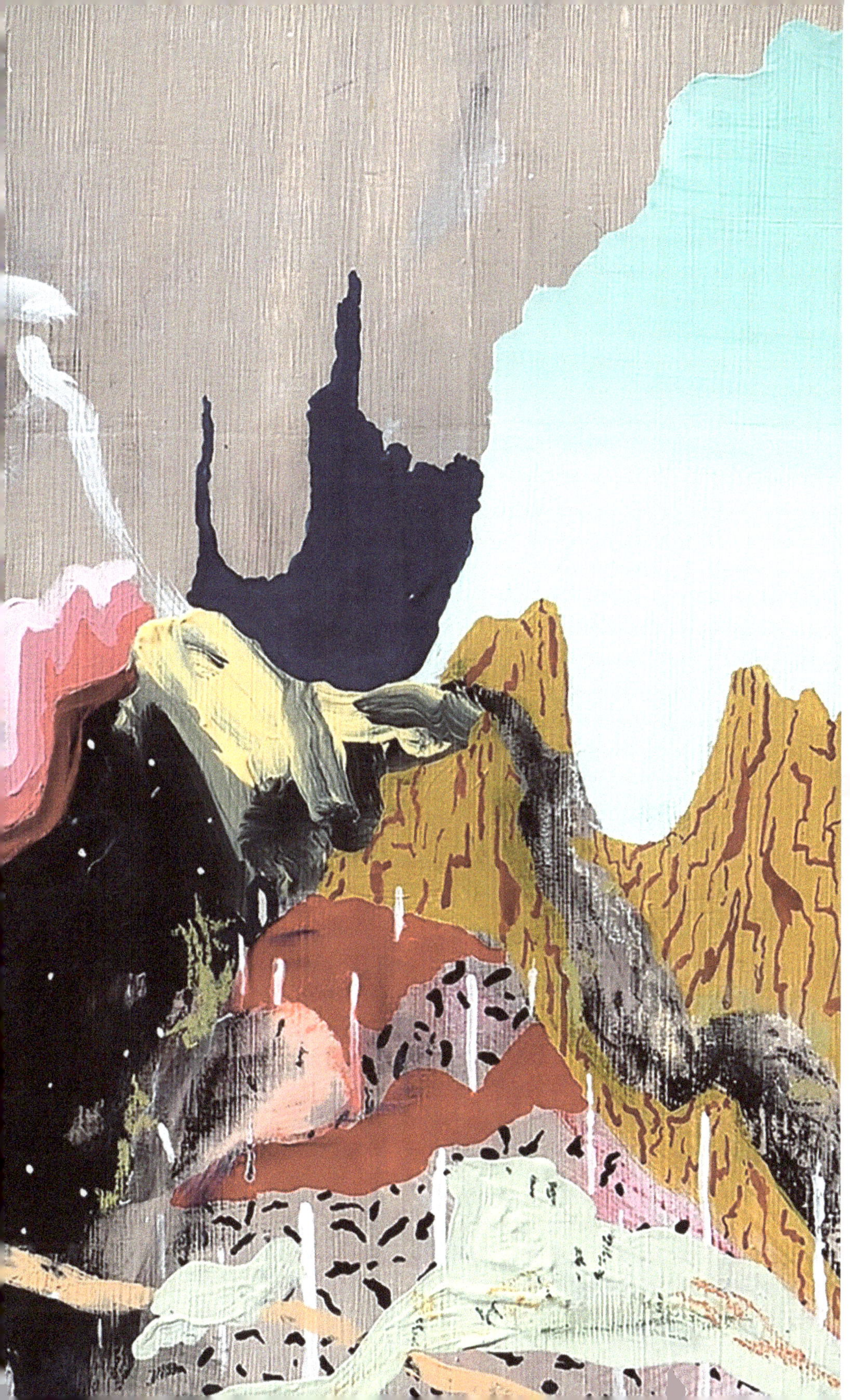

Only after she admitted to knowledge of his fling with Kara, she'd stopped saying it. Maybe it wasn't a conscious decision, but the word dried up. Mary still held him, and kissed, and loved him, Otto assumed. It wasn't the same without the word.

That was why he needed to get clear with her on the money. The money, and whatever today's treat was. No more tender hate. He'd put in notice or quit outright. They'd be okay.

When Otto sidled off the bus, the complaining man followed him.

"So what's wrong with this bucket of bolts?"

"Hopefully nothing. I'll just check, if you don't mind."

"I do mind. I've got business in Tampa. They're bound to promote me. *Paul*, they'll say—"

"Everybody's got business somewhere," intoned Otto, hoping he sound enlightened.

But Paul wouldn't take the hint. He lingered in front of the bus, peering over Otto's shoulder while the driver inspected the engine.

"Seems okay."

"You're wasting our time."

"Just one more thing to check," Otto was saying, languid until Paul shoved him.

"Drive the damn bus!"

Otto stumbled a moment, then recovered himself.

"Okay, sir. I'll—"

Paul pushed again. Otto fell hard, sure the impact meant more than a bruise.

"Listen," he moaned, straining to his feet, his keys dangling from one finger. But his protest got not further. Jaws clenched his legs, like hands held fast in prayer.

Paul's eyes split into two films. The first jerked wildly, an old-time effect for terror and ghosts, as the driver vanished, pulled from the side of the road in a green smear. The second slowed down, a moment where music swells and the audience watches intently for an outcome inevitable as gravity—one that is, in fact, gravity. The keys tumbled from the absent finger and poured slowly to the pavement.

Reflexively, Paul picked them up.

There was nothing to do but straighten corners. After seeing an alligator appear from nowhere, he scuttled to the bus door, hoping the other riders hadn't spotted two men leaving. Maybe they'd find them interchangeable, believing he was the driver.

"Some fellows just wander away. No sense."

Everyone ignored these mutterings, only sighing a bit as the bus did.

Paul recalled his early years on a farm, a thousand miles from Florida, learning to handle a tractor. He was able to control the bus, too. It wasn't the fulfillment of an almost-forgotten dream, happiness reified, but he had business in Tampa, so he kept his eyes forward.

The deal would be worth an awful lot of money.

There might have been questions at the depot, but the passengers seemed as eager as Paul, and when he followed them off the bus, the question of a missing driver belonged to the concrete floor, to plump men with emaciated faces who milled about the place and might be other drivers or other riders, all desperate to leave the hard gray dust of one place, not recognizing life was just as dusty everywhere else.

Silently, Paul laughed at them. He'd made good time, and once in charge of his own car, he reached the downtown skyscraper early.

The client was waiting alone in a conference room. For Paul, this was another win, arriving before his competition. The client's handshake was slow, solemn. Paul kept the smile pasted on his face. He listened to the sad news, that his competitor had died unexpectedly that afternoon. They'd just had word. Still, the deal could move forward.

Paul's smile faded appropriately, and he nodded, thinking this was better than having to negotiate and persuade. He embraced this new, darker self. Here he was, resplendent after decades of striving, with nothing buried, nothing wrapped up and tucked away in the closet. Only today existed.

And today had been different. Since boyhood, every week was part of a furious song and Paul had to fight for what he wanted. Now he was moving up.

He swallowed the client's words.

Yes, he could drive up again in a few days. Bring his partners in love and trade. Or they might take the bus. They were invested, prepared even if business became brutal.

An image was growing in his mind, signs flashing by, of puddles that defy hot days long enough to puff the world before it snaps back and melts.

Honor

Carlton Jackson

Henry Richmond

Michael Munk

Joanne Zuhl

Dan Dobbeck

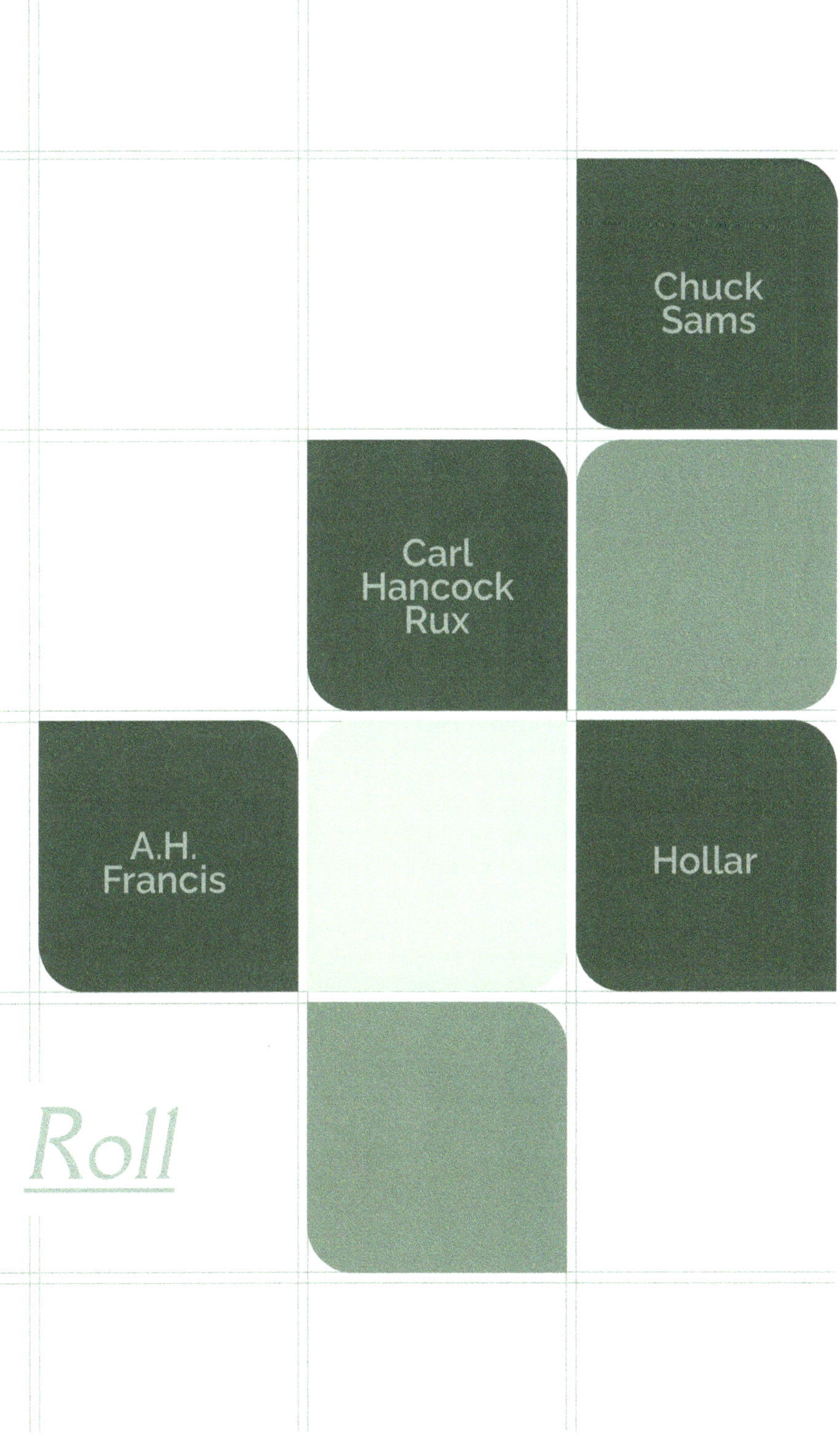
Chuck Sams
Carl Hancock Rux
A.H. Francis
Hollar
Roll

www.ingramcontent.com/pod-product-compliance
Lightning Source LLC
Chambersburg PA
CBHW050030040726
47599CB00015B/1620

* 9 7 8 1 7 3 3 7 2 4 5 7 9 *